For Dad

THE DOOMSDAY FLIGHT

A forgotten Canadian story
by Mark Hagenson

Introduction

In the late 1960s and early '70s, the skies were rife with an unprecedented danger. Airline hijackings occurred, on average, once every five days globally. It was a period that would later be dubbed "the golden age of hijacking," a time when air travel became a high-stakes gamble, and the term "skyjacking" entered the public lexicon.

The covers of major magazines of the time told the story: Newsweek's "The Hijack War," Time's "Pirates in the Sky," and Life's stark "Skyjacking" splashed across newsstands, capturing the zeitgeist of an era gripped by airborne terror.

But amidst the sensational headlines and public panic, there were stories—forgotten events that would remain untold for more than half a century.

This is one such story, based on actual events that started to unfold in the spring of 1966, when the world didn't yet realize the magnitude of the hijacking crisis that lay ahead.

September 21, 1970 / 50 cents
Newsweek
THE HIJACK WAR
SWISSAIR

TIME
Pirates in the Sky

LIFE
The Secret Bobby Fischer
Escape route for a skyjacker—the rear hatch on a Braniff jet. Airline has now sealed hatches on its 727s
SKYJACKING
The get-tough policy could make it even worse
AUGUST 11 · 1972 · 50¢

Chapter 1: Night Jump

April 18, 1966 - Somewhere over Fort Benning Army Training Base, Georgia, USA

The night sky was a vast, inky canvas, punctuated only by the faint twinkle of stars and the imposing silhouette of a Lockheed C-130 Hercules aircraft. Its four propellers thrumming a steady beat at 125 knots. Inside the plane's cavernous hold, bathed in an eerie green glow, twenty-six men stood in various states of anxious anticipation. Among them, fifteenth in line, was Paul Joseph Cini.

At twenty-two years old, the youthful Cini was tempered by military discipline. His face was set in grim determination, though none could see it clearly in the dim light. His Army fatigues, adorned with patches declaring his name and allegiance to both the U.S. Army and its 101st Airborne division, seemed to weigh heavily on his frame. It wasn't just the physical burden of his equipment that bore down on him, but the weight of the moment—the knowledge that in mere minutes, he would be hurtling through the air at 1,200 feet above the ground.

The air was thick with the smell of sweat and metal, underscored by the persistent drone of the aircraft's engines. Cini's fingers moved restlessly, checking and rechecking his gear. Each buckle, strap, and clasp demanded his attention, a ritual born of training and fear in equal measure.

Suddenly, the Jump Master's voice cut through the din, sharp and authoritative: "Hook up!"

In a synchronized dance, the paratroopers snapped their yellow static lines into the overhead anchor cable. The sound of metal clasping metal rang out, a staccato symphony of commitment. There was no turning back now.

With a grunt of effort, the Jump Master turned the large yellow handle of the exit door counter clockwise a quarter turn and slid it up vertically on the inside of the C-130. A wall of sound crashed into the cargo hold. A gust of wind howled into the compartment, bringing with it the full, terrifying roar of the engines and the realization of the vast emptiness waiting outside. The sound drowning out everything but the pounding of Cini's heart in his ears.

"Check equipment!" the Jump Master bellowed over the cacophony.

"Set!" The paratroopers' response was a unified shout, a testament to their training and the bonds forged in preparation for moments like these.

As the Jump Master received last-minute information through his headset, Cini felt his heart hammering against his ribs. The tinny words filtered through from the flight deck to the waiting men: "Winds southwest 10 gusting to 20. 30 seconds to DZ."

"30 seconds!" The call was repeated down by the paratroopers in unison "30 seconds!" A countdown to the moment of truth.

The Jump Master fist bumps the first paratrooper in line. "Stand in the door!" he hollered.

Cini watched as the paratrooper took his position at the door, the red light near the opening casting an ominous glow. The rest of the line moved forward shuffling their feet to close up the space between them. The final seconds ticked away, each one feeling like an eternity.

The flight deck started to countdown from 5 to the Jump Master which he repeated to the paratroopers "5, 4, 3, 2..."

The red light blinked out, replaced by bright green. "Green light! Go, go, go!"

One by one, the men ahead of Cini disappeared into the night, each departure punctuated by the Jump Master's relentless command: "Go!"

As Cini inched closer to the door, his breath came in ragged gasps. The wind tore at his clothes, and the yawning blackness beyond the aircraft seemed to beckon. When his turn came, he hesitated for a fraction of a second—a moment of human frailty in the face of the dark void.

Finally he handed his yellow static line to the Jump Master and with shouted "Go!" ringing in his ears, he plummeted into the abyss.

The world spun, a dizzying kaleidoscope of stars and shadows. For three heart-stopping seconds, Cini fell, his body buffeted by the rushing air. Then, with a violent jolt that rattled every bone in his body, his parachute deployed. The abrupt deceleration snapped him upright, and suddenly, the chaos of the fall gave way to an eerie serenity.

Suspended between heaven and earth, Cini turned his gaze upward. The near-full moon hung low and heavy in the sky, casting its pale light over the surreal scene. In the distance, six other C-130s droned in harmony, their formation growing ever smaller as they flew off into the distance. All around him, dozens of ghostly silhouettes drifted slowly earthward. Fellow paratroopers now scattered across the night sky like dandelion seeds in a gentle breeze.

As he floated down towards the unseen ground, he couldn't have known that this night—this jump—was merely the prelude to events that would change the course of his life forever. The true test of his mettle lay not in this momentary fall through darkness, but in the turbulent skies of a future yet to unfold.

Chapter 2: A Life Unraveling

August 15, 1971 - Calgary, Alberta, Canada

The morning sun cast a harsh light through the windows of the modest suburban home. Inside, the day was already spiraling into familiar patterns of tension and unspoken resentments.

In the bedroom closet, a US Army Airborne uniform hung forgotten, gathering dust—a silent reminder of a life left behind. Pamela, 27, stood in the ensuite bathroom, carefully applying her makeup. Her movements were precise, controlled, a stark contrast to the turmoil that seemed to be engulfing their lives.

Meanwhile, in the kitchen, Paul Cini, now 27, sat at a small square table. The clock on the wall ticked steadily towards 10:22am, each second seeming to mock the stagnation that had settled over his life. The newspaper before him was spread open, but his attention was divided between the headlines and the drink he was preparing. With practiced ease, he poured three fingers of vodka into a tall glass, topping it off with orange juice. A screwdriver—his breakfast of champions.

A small portable TV hummed in the background, transitioning from the weather forecast to a grim report on the ongoing conflict in Northern Ireland. Cini took a long pull from his drink, his eyes flicking between the TV and the newspaper.

"In the Ballymurphy area of West Belfast, Northern Ireland," the newscaster's voice droned, "at least 11 innocent people have been killed by British Army paratroopers in what some are calling a massacre. They were there to arrest IRA suspects without trial."

Cini's gaze fell to the newspaper, where a similar story screamed from the page: "13 KILLED AS NEW WAVE OF FURY ENGULFS NORTHERN IRELAND TOWN." The details were even more chilling in print—two women, a priest, a 15-year-old boy, and seven other civilians among the dead.

A low growl escaped Cini's throat as he clenched his fist, his knuckles white with tension. Almost unconsciously, he began to scratch at the backs of his hands, a nervous habit that had grown more pronounced in recent months.

The TV shifted to another story, one that captured Cini's full attention. A hijacking out of Acapulco, Mexico. He leaned forward, taking a gulp from his morning cocktail as he absorbed every detail.

"On Friday July 2nd, Braniff Flight 14, a Boeing 707 flying from Acapulco to New York with 102 passengers and a crew of eight, was hijacked on approach to a refueling stop in San Antonio, Texas," the reporter explained. "The ordeal lasted 43 hours traversing Texas, Mexico, Peru, Brazil and ending in Argentina. After a refueling stop in Monterrey, the hijackers released the flight attendants and all of the passengers. The remaining crew of Captain Dale Bessant, Bill Wallace, Phillip Wray and flight attendants Ernestina Garcia and Margaret Susan Harris flew on to Lima, Peru. The hijackers, a U.S. Navy deserter named Robert Jackson and his Guatemalan lady friend, demanded and got a ransom of $100,000. They demanded passage to Algeria."

Cini couldn't believe what he was hearing.

The reporter continued, "The 707 left for Rio and planned to refuel for the long flight to Algiers, but the hijacker forced them on to Buenos Aires. The long flight and fatigue took its toll and it was there that the hijackers gave up. It was a record for long-distance hijacking, over 7,500 miles."

The story unfolded like a Hollywood thriller—43 hours of terror, spanning multiple countries, a ransom of $100,000, and a record-breaking 7,500-mile journey. As Cini listened, he was overcome with a mix of emotions. Fascination, envy, and something darker, more dangerous. His mind raced with possibilities, calculations, what-ifs...

"So what's the plan, Paul?" Pamela's voice, sharp with frustration, cut through his reverie. "It's been over 4 months since your last delivery job. You need to find something today. Our savings are almost gone, and my mother isn't going to bail us out again."

The words hit Cini like a physical blow. In an instant, the simmering tension that had been building all morning erupted. He slammed both fists on the table, the impact sending tremors through his half-empty glass. In one fluid motion, he stood, the chair scraping loudly against the linoleum floor, downed the remainder of his "juice," and snatched his keys from the counter.

The front door slammed behind him shaking the entire house and leaving a ringing silence in its wake. A punctuation mark to the frustration and aimlessness that had come to define his life.

As Cini stormed out into the bright Calgary morning, the seeds of desperation were already taking root. The man who had once jumped from planes with pride and purpose now felt himself in a free fall, with no parachute in sight.

The morning sun glinted off the hood of his blue 1968 GMC delivery utility step-van, a remnant of better days when he'd had steady work. Cini yanked open the driver's side door and slid behind the wheel, his movements fueled by frustration and restless energy. As he turned the key in the ignition, the radio crackled to life, filling the van with the chorus of "No Time" by The Guess Who.

Seasons change and so did I
You need not wonder why
You need not wonder why
There's no time left for you
No time left for you

The lyrics seemed to mock him as he peeled out of the driveway, tires squealing against the asphalt. Cini found himself unconsciously tapping the steering wheel as he made his way down Macleod Trail, the familiar sights of Calgary blurring past his windows. As he drove, his mind kept returning to the hijacking story. The audacity of it, the thrill, the potential payoff. For a man with nothing left to lose, it was a dangerous line of thought.

Chapter 3: A Dangerous Plan

Just minutes from his home, the neon sign of O'Shea's Bar caught his eye. Despite the early hour, Cini felt an irresistible pull towards the establishment. He veered into the nearly empty parking lot, the van's tires crunching on loose gravel.

As Cini approached the entrance, Shelagh O'Shea, the 32-year-old owner-operator, was unlocking the heavy carved wooden door from the inside. Her face, framed by auburn curls, lit up with recognition as she swung the door open.

"Oh hey Paul! 'Top o' the mornin'," Shelagh greeted him, her slight Irish accent a sort of comforting reminder of home. Paul was born in Scotland. "You're here a trifle early today, darlin'. Come on in."

"Hiya Shelagh, thanks," Cini replied, following her into the dim interior of the bar.

The familiar scent of stale beer, cigarettes and polished wood enveloped him as they made their way to the long, curved bar. Cini settled onto a worn leather bar stool while Shelagh took her place behind the counter, surrounded by an eclectic collection of UK pub memorabilia. Irish beer and whiskey signs adorned every available surface, creating a slice of the Emerald Isle in the heart of Calgary.

"The usual, hon?" Shelagh asked, reaching for a bottle.

Cini shook his head. "Nah, I think I'll have a barley sandwich this morning, love."

With a knowing smile, Shelagh grabbed an old-school '70s era glass stein and started a foamy pour from the single Labatt's Draught handle. She had to pour off a good amount of foam before presenting Cini with a respectable pint, placing it on a cardboard coaster in front of him.

Cini took a long pull, savouring the crisp, bitter taste. He wiped the creamy white head off his upper lip with the back of his wrist before broaching the subject that had been weighing on his mind.

"Have you heard from your brother yet?" he asked, his tone careful.

Shelagh's face fell as she busied herself with getting the bar ready for the day. "No, not yet. We're all really worried about Tommy. Mum thinks he's most likely ended up in one of those British internment camps in Belfast..." She paused, her voice dropping to a near whisper. "Me?... I'm just hoping he's still alive. I knew it was just a matter of time before something was going to happen to him after he joined the IRA."

Cini shook his head, anger bubbling up inside him. "Aagh. Did you hear about that massacre in Ballymurphy over there? It's awful. Women, children. A priest even. I can understand why he joined. These pommy bastards are ruthless."

"So sad," Shelagh agreed, wiping down the bar with more force than necessary. "I feel helpless with all of this nonsense going on back home and not being able to do anything about it."

Cini leaned in, his voice low and intense. "What if I told you that I think there is?"

Shelagh raised an eyebrow, intrigued. "I'm listening."

Cini glanced around the empty bar before continuing in a hushed tone. "I've decided that I want to raise some quick money for the cause. They need cash for weapons and recruits to combat these thugs. The quickest and easiest way that I can figure to do that is to hijack a loaded airliner for ransom."

Shelagh's mouth dropped open in shock. "...that's crazy Paul," she whispered loudly. "Even if you could get them to give you the cash, how could you possibly get away?"

A hint of a smile played at the corners of Cini's mouth. "That's the beauty of my plan, you see. I jump out of the plane never to be seen again and nobody gets hurt. Time to put my 101st Airborne training to good use."

"Parachute!?" Shelagh exclaimed, shaking her head in disbelief. "You're completely mad!" She grabs his hands and pulls herself closer. "But… I like it. You're gonna need some help, love." She took a sip from her coffee, her mind already racing with the possibilities.

Cini nodded, his expression growing serious. "Yeah. I know." He leaned in even closer, his voice barely audible. "*I need dynamite.*"

Shelagh nearly choked on her coffee. "*Dynamite!?!* Where the hell are you going to dig that up?"

"That's exactly what I was going to ask you," Cini replied. "What about your brother's connection up in Edmonton?"

"The Malloy Gang?" Shelagh's eyes widened. "Jesus Paul, I haven't spoken to Declan and the boys for ages." She paused, considering. "But they do actually owe us a favour or two. Tell you what, let me see what I can do. If I ask nicely, I'm sure they would be happy to help."

Cini nodded, relief washing over him. "OK. Make it happen. Don't call the house though. I don't want Pam catching wind of this. There's some other pieces to this puzzle I need to track down. In the meantime, you just take care of yourself and keep your chin up."

He downed the last of his beer and slapped some change on the bar. As he stood to leave, Cini locked eyes with Shelagh. "Tiocfaidh ár lá," he said solemnly.

"Tiocfaidh ár lá, Paul," Shelagh replied, the familiar Irish phrase—"Our time will come"—hanging in the air between them.

As the door swung shut behind Cini, Shelagh reached for a bottle of Jameson. She poured a couple of glugs into a rocks glass and took a big gulp, steadying her nerves. With a deep breath, she pulled down a little black book wedged between bottles on the back wall. Her fingers trembled slightly as she flipped it open and picked up the rotary wall phone, dialing a number she hadn't called in years.

The phone rang once, twice, before a gruff voice answered. "Yes?"

Shelagh swallowed hard. "It's Shelagh O'Shea, Decco. We need a hand."

As Shelagh began explaining the situation to her old contact, a sense of unease settled over her. She couldn't shake the feeling that her actions today might have far-reaching consequences. Outside, the sound of Cini's van faded into the distance, carrying with it the weight of their newly hatched plan.

Chapter 4: Preparations

As Cini guided his blue van through the streets of Calgary, his mind raced with the details of his audacious plan. The conversation with Shelagh had crystallized his intentions, transforming vague notions into concrete steps. Now, it was time to gather the tools he'd need. The afternoon sun beat down on the parking lot of the Army & Navy store as he pulled in and parked. He stepped out, the van's engine ticking as it cooled. Taking a deep breath, he walked calmly towards the entrance, just another shopper on a mundane errand. In reality, it was a gateway to the next phase of his audacious plan.

Inside, the fluorescent lights cast a harsh glow over the aisles of military surplus and outdoor gear. Cini grabbed a shopping cart, its wobbly wheel squeaking in protest as he navigated the store with purpose. His eyes scanned the shelves, ticking off a mental checklist.

A folding shovel. Leather gloves. Flashlight. Water canteen. Rope. Pup tent. Buck knife. Twine. Each item found its way into the cart, pieces of a puzzle only Cini could see. He paused in the clothing aisle, his gaze settling on a rack of oversized beige trench coats. Slipping one on he turned to examine his reflection in a nearby mirror and nodded to himself.

"Perfect," he muttered, tossing the coat into the cart.

At the checkout, Cini unloaded his haul onto the conveyor belt. The young checkout girl, barely out of her teens, raised an eyebrow at the eclectic mix of survival gear. Cini met her gaze with a casual smile, then grabbed a handful of candy and chocolate bars from the display, tossing them onto the belt as an afterthought.

As the mechanical cash register clattered and pinged, tallying up his purchases, Cini's mind wandered to the next item on his list. The most crucial piece of equipment he'd need for his daring escape.

Back in the van, Cini consulted a scrap of paper with an address scribbled on it. Before long, he found himself pulling into the parking lot of the Calgary Skydiving School. In the distance, a tandem skydive pair touched down in a large field, their colorful canopy fluttering to the ground. The sight sent a jolt of adrenaline through him, a vivid reminder of his days with the 101st Airborne.

The office of the skydiving school was a cramped space, its walls adorned with an array of gear for sale. As Cini entered, browsing the merchandise with feigned casualness, a woman behind the desk looked up from her paperwork.

"Is there anything I can help you find?" she asked, her voice cheerful but professional.

Cini turned to her, his expression neutral. "I'm looking for a parachute."

The clerk gestured towards the far wall. "All our parachutes for sale are over there. What type are you looking for?"

"Nothing fancy," Cini replied, his tone carefully nonchalant. "Just a regular old round one. What's your cheapest?"

The woman pointed to a lower shelf. "That would be the red and yellow striped one at the bottom. $199. Includes the harness."

Cini frowned slightly. "Don't you have something in plain blue or black?"

"Only in a ram air model," she explained, "and those start at $500 without a harness."

For a moment, Cini hesitated. The brightly colored chute would be far from ideal for his purposes, but the price difference was significant. Making a quick decision, he grabbed the red and yellow parachute and harness, placing them on the counter with a thud.

"I guess I can dye it myself," he said, a hint of resignation in his voice. "I'll take it."

As the clerk rang up his purchase, Cini's mind raced. This wasn't just a parachute he was buying; it was his ticket to freedom. Now he had the essentials – the tools he'd need to pull off his daring plan.

Leaving the skydiving school with his new purchase, Cini felt a mix of exhilaration and apprehension. The weight of the parachute in his arms was a stark reminder of the reality of what he was planning. There would be no turning back now.

As he loaded the parachute into his van, Cini glanced around the parking lot, suddenly acutely aware of his surroundings. Did anyone suspect what he was planning? Could they see the determination – or was it desperation? – in his eyes?

Shaking off his paranoia, Cini climbed back into the driver's seat. He had more preparations to make, more pieces to gather. Those pieces were falling into place, but the most dangerous parts of his scheme still lay ahead. As he drove home, his mind whirled with the remaining tasks: obtaining the dynamite through Shelagh's contacts, planning the hijacking itself, and figuring out how to get the money to the IRA.

The sun was beginning to set as Cini pulled into his driveway, casting long shadows across the neighborhood. He'd have to hide his purchases from Pamela, make up some story about picking up extra work. As he unloaded the van, carefully concealing the parachute beneath the other supplies, Cini couldn't shake the feeling that he had crossed a point of no return.

His path was set now, for better or worse. All that remained was to see it through to the end, whatever that might be.

Chapter 5: Takeoff

The crisp autumn air at Vancouver International Airport carried the distinct smell of jet fuel with a hint of sea salt from the nearby Pacific. Outside the domestic departures terminal Mary Dohey, a 38-year-old veteran Air Canada stewardess, stepped off the shuttle bus. Her company issued blue-grey overcoat fluttered in the cool breeze, white scarf and gloves completing her professional ensemble. With her carry-on bag slung over one shoulder and purse on the other, she approached the sliding glass doors which opened automatically with a soft hiss.

Inside the bustling terminal, the familiar sights and sounds of the airport enveloped her. The click-clack of dress shoes on polished floors, the murmur of conversations in multiple languages, and the occasional crackle of announcements over the PA system created a symphony of travel that Mary had come to love over her years of service.

As she made her way through the terminal, eyes scanning the crowd, a familiar face caught her eye. A smile lit up her face. John Arpin, the 48-year-old purser, was already there, his experienced gaze surveying the morning crowd. Mary quickened her pace, catching up to him with a playful hip bump.

"Hey!" John's face breaking into a warm grin. "I didn't expect to see you here. Are you on 812?"

Mary nodded, rolling her eyes good-naturedly. "Yeah, I'm filling in for Helen. Some kind of sniffles again."

John chuckled, giving her a friendly shoulder hug. "Well, just between you and me, you're a lot more fun on these cross-country hop, skip, and jump flights than she is. Good to see you!"

As they made their way through the terminal, John filled her in on the flight plan. "Quick stops in Calgary and YYZ, and we'll be back in Montreal in no time, Mary."

"I just hope it wasn't as bumpy as last week," Mary replied with a slight grimace. "Felt like we were in a martini shaker going over the Rockies."

After passing through the security checkpoint, they watched as Captain Vern Ehman and First Officer Nels Hagenson bypassed the line of passengers, casually passing through the metal detector. The two pilots, aged 43 and 30 respectively, exuded an air of confidence that came from years of experience in the cockpit.

The two pilots joined Mary, John, and Second Officer Noel Belanger. As the crew made their way down the jet bridge, their conversation was a mix of small talk and inside jokes that spoke of long hours spent together in the confines of aircraft cabins and distant hotel rooms.

Stepping into the cabin of Flight 812, a gleaming state of the art McDonnell Douglas DC-8 jetliner, they were greeted by Anna-Mae Smith, a young stewardess in her early 20's already on board. She took the cockpit crew's overcoats, hanging them up as the pilots settled into their domain.

In the cockpit, the crew started flicking switches and twisting knobs. Captain Ehman's voice took on the authoritative tone of a man in his element. "OK boys, time to get down to business. You want to run through the pre-start checklist, Nels?"

"Sure." First Officer Hagenson pulled out a kneepad checklist with sliders. "Parking brake."

"Set," Captain Ehman responded.

"Throttle."

"Idle."

"Fuel flow."

"Cutoff," said Second Officer Belanger from the seat behind the first officer facing a literal wall filled with gauges, knobs and switches.

As Hagenson continued the familiar litany of the pre-flight checklist, Mary and John turned their attention to welcoming the passengers.

As the last few passengers boarded a mother and her young daughter, Hannah, caught Mary's attention. The girl's nervousness was palpable, her small hand clutching her mother's tightly. Mary's nurturing instincts kicked in immediately. "Welcome aboard Flight 812. Where are we off to?"

"We're going to Montreal to visit Hannah's grandparents," the mother replied handing Mary their boarding passes. "She's also excited to try real poutine for the first time."

"Well you're going to the right place for that Hannah. I'm Mary and this is John."

Mary knelt down to Hannah's eye level. "Is this your first time flying?" she asked gently.

Hannah nodded "Uh huh", her eyes wide.

"She's a little nervous," said mom.

"Nervous? Well, let me put your mind at ease sweetie."

With a reassuring smile, Mary pulled back the curtain hiding the cockpit. "Up there in the cockpit we have three of Air Canada's finest pilots, including the legendary Captain Vern Ehman. They have thousands and thousands of hours of flying experience. This DC-8 jetliner you're on is one of the most advanced and safest aircraft in the world. You're in very good hands and have nothing to worry about."

The mother mouthed a silent "thank you" as Hannah's eyes widened with wonder at the glimpse into the cockpit. Mary winked at the mother and added, "Hey, I've got an idea. Would you like to go up to the cockpit and say hi to the fellas a bit later?"

Hannah's face lit up, her earlier nervousness forgotten. "Uh-huh!"

"Sounds like a plan," Mary said. "Once we've taken off and are at altitude I'll come back and take you guys up ok?"

"OK!" Hannah exclaimed grinning ear to ear.

"Well then, it looks like you guys are in row 21 seats A and B. So just head towards the back of the plane and you're on the right. Make sure you get the window seat Hannah. We're going to be going over the Rocky Mountains which is really neat."

"Thank you for your help," mom said.

"No problem. We'll see you soon. Anna-Mae is your stewardess back there. Just let her know if you need anything."

As Mary directed them toward their seats she couldn't help but feel a surge of pride in her job. These small moments, helping passengers feel safe and excited about their journey, were what made the long hours and occasional turbulence worthwhile.

With the last passengers seated, John pulled the massive exit door closed, locking it with the two-foot-long lever. "Doors armed and cross-checked," he reported to the cockpit via the galley intercom.

In the cockpit, the pre-flight routine continued, a well-choreographed dance of switches flicked and knobs twisted. As Captain Ehman, First Officer Hagenson, and Second Officer Belanger ran through their checks, their conversation drifted to personal catch-up.

 "By the way, a hearty welcome back to Vancouver, Nels," Ehman said. "It's been a while. How long were you gone? I don't think I've seen you in at least two years."

"Sounds about right," First Officer Hagenson replied, adjusting his headset. "Time flies when you're having fun though."

Ehman's eyes crinkled with interest. "So how was your recent stint with Air Jamaica? That was lucky to be picked up as a loaner pilot after the merger for a guy your age." He grinned mischievously. "I hear the girls in Kingston are pretty feisty."

Hagenson chuckled, his face brightening at the memory. "I had a couple of dates, Vern. Although they generally had us in and out of there lickety split." He shook his head ruefully. "Some layovers I was lucky if I was able to get a Tastee beef patty from one of their food trucks." His expression grew wistful. "Man, those things are addictive. Spicy."

"Well, at least it's a healthy addiction," Ehman said. "Those are good. I was there with Margaret a few years back. I remember how crystal clear the water is down there." He paused, curious. "I trust you at least got to do some snorkeling at some point."

Hagenson was writing on his notepad, periodically glancing at the readouts on the center console. His voice took on an animated tone as he replied, "Oh yeah. Actually when I was on days off I got SCUBA certified while I was down there." His eyes lit up with enthusiasm. "The Throne Room off of Negril is unbelievable. There's these incredible coral formations. Stingrays, eels, octopus. I even saw a couple of nurse sharks." He smiled in remembrance. "Magnificent creatures those. Fearsome looking but very docile."

Turning his head toward the rear of the cockpit, Hagenson called out, "How about you, Noel? What's the latest?"

Second Officer Belanger's voice carried a note of self-deprecating humor. "Unfortunately I cannot report on anything quite as adventurous as that, Nels. I'm just happy to be waking up on the green side of the grass, sir."

The three men shared a hearty laugh, the sound filling the confined space of the cockpit. The moment of camaraderie was broken by Captain Ehman's return to business. "You and me both, my friend." His voice took on a more professional tone. "Alright boys, let's get this bird off the ground. Give us the rest of the checklist, Nels."

Hagenson's eyes dropped to the checklist resting on his lap. "Roger, Captain."

"Nav lights."

"On"

"Taxi lights."

"On."

Outside, ground crews bustled around the massive DC-8, making final preparations for its journey across the country. The hose was unhooked from the fuel truck before it drove off.

Finally, with all checks complete and clearance received from the tower, Captain Ehman's voice came over the intercom, steady and reassuring. "Ladies and gentlemen, this is your captain speaking. We're cleared for pushback and should be airborne in just a few minutes. Please ensure your seatbelts are fastened and all carry-on items are properly stowed. We're looking at clear skies ahead, and our flight time to Calgary today will be approximately one hour and fifteen minutes. Sit back, relax, and enjoy the flight."

Captain Ehman's voice crackled over the radio. "Air Canada 812, ready for pushback."

As the ground crew began to maneuver the massive DC-8 away from the gate, the familiar sensation of movement rippled through the cabin. Outside, the late afternoon sun glinted off the plane's polished fuselage, the Air Canada logo on the tail a proud emblem against the sky.

Vancouver ground control radioed the crew "Air Canada 812 cleared to runway 08 via taxiway Juliette. Hold short runway 08."

As the DC-8 approached runway 08, a massive Pan Am Boeing 747 landed. "Clipper Pride of the Sea" is emblazoned across the front part of her fuselage. Once it had taxied off, Flight 812 proceeded to line up on runway 08. Air traffic control radioed "Air Canada 812 cleared for takeoff runway heading to 7000." The engines roared to life as both Captain Lehman and FO Hagenson placed their hands on the throttle quadrant one on top of another and pushed it slowly to full thrust. The DC-8 began to lumber down the runway gathering speed.

Monitoring their speed, Hagenson said "V1" and a few seconds later "Rotate."

Captain Lehman pulled back on the control column and they were airborne.

"Gear up."

The four main gear legs and nose leg retracted into the body of the sleek jet and its 18 wheels disappeared into the fuselage. Mary glanced out a nearby window. The sprawling industrial suburb of Richmond gave way to the snow-capped North Shore mountains and the glittering expanse of Vancouver City. It was a view she never tired of, a reminder of the beauty and vastness of the country they were about to traverse.

Little did Mary, or any of the crew and passengers of Flight 812, know that their routine journey was about to become anything but ordinary. As the DC-8 climbed into the clear blue sky, leaving Vancouver behind, it carried not just its manifest of crew and passengers, but also the weight of impending danger that none of them could yet foresee. The seeds of Paul Cini's desperate plan were already taking root, set to intersect with the lives of everyone on board Flight 812.

Chapter 6: Uneasy Skies

As Flight 812 climbed to its cruising altitude, a soft "bong" sound echoed throughout the cabin, accompanied by the fasten seatbelt sign going dark. John and Mary, released from their jump seats, made their way to the first-class galley. The familiar routine of preparing drinks and snacks began, but there was an undercurrent of tension that John couldn't help but notice.

"You're looking a little pale, Mary. Are you feeling okay?" John asked, his eyes searching her face with concern.

Mary forced a smile. "I'm fine, John. Just a little tired, that's all."

But John wasn't convinced. "Are you sure? You're not feeling sick, are you?"

Mary shook her head, her hands busying themselves with arranging glasses on a tray. "No, no, I'm not sick. I just... I don't know. I have this weird feeling."

John, trying to lighten the mood, grinned. "Well, up there in the cockpit, like you said to little Hannah, we have three of Air Canada's finest pilots. You have nothing to worry about." He paused for effect. "Well, maybe except for that First Officer Nels. Been known to be a bit of a ladies' man."

Mary punched him lightly on the shoulder, a genuine laugh escaping her. "Harhar. Very funny." But the moment of levity passed quickly, and her expression grew serious again. "I don't know what it is, John. I just have this strange, uneasy feeling." She shook her head as if trying to clear it. "I'll be fine."

John's teasing smile softened into one of genuine concern. "Alright. Well, let me know if you need a hug or something."

"Will do," Mary replied, grateful for her colleague's support.

As they continued their preparations, Mary couldn't shake the nagging sense of foreboding. She'd flown countless times before, weathered turbulence and difficult passengers, but this feeling was different. It was as if a shadow had passed over the sun, leaving a chill she couldn't quite explain. Outside the small galley windows, the vast expanse of the Canadian wilderness stretched out below them, the approaching Rocky Mountains a snow-capped barrier on the horizon.

Meanwhile, in the cockpit, an entirely different atmosphere prevailed. Mary had taken Hannah, the young girl Mary had comforted earlier, and her mother up to the cockpit about 20 minutes earlier. Hannah was deep in conversation with the flight crew, her earlier nervousness replaced by wide-eyed wonder.

"Well, it was very nice to meet you, Hannah," First Officer Hagenson said leaning back in his seat, clearly impressed. "Keep up with your fact-finding. I had no idea that a bird could possibly fly as high as we are now at 37,000 feet. What kind of vulture did you say it was?"

Hannah's eyes lit up with enthusiasm. "It's called a Rüppell's Vulture. It's named after Eduard Rüppell. He was a German naturalist and explorer from the 1800s."

Captain Ehman chuckled, shaking his head in amazement. "Wow. You really know your stuff." He glanced at his instruments, then back at Hannah and her mother. "We're just about to head over the Rockies and start our descent into Calgary. You and your mom better get back to your seat." With a wink, he added, "Keep an eye out for one of them vultures!"

"I will. Thank you!" Hannah beamed, her earlier fear of flying completely forgotten.

As Mary led Hannah and her mother back to their seats, she couldn't help but smile at the girl's excitement. It was moments like these that reminded her why she loved her job, despite the occasional bouts of unease.

Back in the cockpit, Hagenson watched them go. "What a bright girl," he remarked.

Ehman nodded in agreement. "Indeed." Then, shifting back into his professional demeanor, he addressed his crew. "Alright, fellas, let's head on down to Cowtown."

As the DC-8 began its gradual descent towards Calgary, the majestic Rocky Mountains loomed closer. The late afternoon sun cast on the rugged landscape created a breathtaking vista that even the most seasoned crew members couldn't help but admire.

In the passenger cabin, excited murmurs and the clicks of camera shutters filled the air as travelers pressed their faces to the windows, eager to capture the stunning scenery. Hannah, true to the captain's suggestion, scanned the skies intently, hoping for a glimpse of a high-flying vulture.

Back in the galley, Mary tried to focus on her tasks, but the unsettling feeling persisted. She found herself glancing nervously at the passengers, searching for... what? She couldn't say. Everything seemed normal, yet something felt off.

Little did Mary know that her intuition was picking up on the invisible threads of fate that were drawing them all towards an encounter that would test their courage, skills, and humanity in ways they could never have imagined. Far below, in a nondescript house in Calgary, Paul Cini was making his final preparations. The paths of Flight 812 and Cini's desperate plan were about to intersect. The clock was ticking down to a moment that would change all their lives forever.

Chapter 7: The Passenger

As the afternoon sun cast long shadows across Calgary International Airport, Paul Cini stood at the Air Canada departure counter, his oversized beige trench coat hanging loosely on his frame. In one hand, he clutched a plastic Woolco department store shopping bag, its contents hidden by silver duct tape wrapped tightly around it. His eyes darted nervously to the blue suitcase on the scale before him, then back to the young counter attendant.

"Your flight will begin boarding in about 15 minutes at Gate 12, Mr. Munro," the attendant said cheerfully, handing over his tickets and boarding pass. "Enjoy your flight."

Cini snatched the documents without a word, his lips pressed into a thin line. He turned abruptly, nearly bumping into another traveller, and strode purposefully down the busy concourse.

As he approached a crossroads, a large sign caught his attention:

<<-- DOMESTIC GATES 1-12　　US / INTERNATIONAL GATES 13-24 -->>

Just then, the PA system crackled to life:

"Please be aware that at this time all US and international passengers departing from gates 13 through 24 will be passing through our new metal detector screening system. Kindly remove all metallic items from your person such as belts, keys, rings and watches and place them in the screening bins."

Cini glanced at his boarding pass: "Gate 12 Seat 2B". With a slight exhale of relief, he turned left towards the domestic gates. In his haste, he collided with a woman holding hands with a young boy, causing her to spill her coffee all over her white overcoat.

"Hey! Watch where you're going!" the woman exclaimed, her face flushed with anger.

"Fuck you" Cini muttered under his breath, not bothering to slow his pace or look back. He could feel the boy's disapproving gaze boring into his back as he walked away.

At Gate 12, Cini handed his boarding pass to John, who gave it a cursory glance before motioning him down the gangway. As Cini stepped onto the plane, he was greeted by Anna-Mae and Mary, their professional smiles unwavering despite his brusque demeanor.

"You're just here in 2B," Anna-Mae said, gesturing towards his seat. "May I take your coat?"

"No," Cini growled. "Later."

He settled into his seat, still wearing his coat, acutely aware of the curious glances from other first-class passengers. The man behind him in 3B offered a friendly "Hello" but Cini ignored him, placing his parcel on the floor and began to scratch at the backs of his hands.

As the aircraft began to taxi, John's voice came over the PA system, welcoming passengers and providing safety instructions.

"Good afternoon ladies and gentlemen once again welcome aboard Air Canada Flight 812. My name is John Arpin and I am the purser on this flight. Myself and the rest of the crew are happy to be serving you today enroute to Montreal with a quick stopover in Toronto.

In preparation for takeoff please ensure that all luggage is stowed either under the seat in front of you or in the overhead compartments.

This McDonnell Douglas DC-8 aircraft is equipped with 4 lavatories, two at the rear of the plane and two in the first class section. The two in first class are reserved exclusively for those passengers and, for security reasons, we appreciate your cooperation and understanding as you help us respect this arrangement.

Please remain seated with your seatbelt on anytime the fasten seatbelt sign is on. When the Captain turns the sign off, that will be your indication that it's safe to move about the cabin. We ask that you also please keep your seatbelt fastened at all times while seated. Soon we will begin our service this afternoon. Until then please sit back, relax and enjoy the flight. Thank you for choosing Air Canada."

The familiar routine of the pre-flight announcements washed over Cini, barely registering as he focused on controlling his breathing and steadying his nerves.

The takeoff was smooth, the DC-8 lifting into the golden glow of the Canadian prairie autumn just as the sun began to set. Once at cruising altitude, John started the beverage service for first class. He placed a small square Air Canada cocktail napkin and a pack of peanuts on Cini's tray table.

"Would you like something to drink?" John asked politely.

"A Screwdriver," Cini replied gruffly. "Make it a double and make it snappy."

As John retreated to the galley, Cini's agitation grew. He fumbled with the pack of peanuts, unable to open it. In a burst of frustration, he threw it against the fuselage, causing the package to explode and scatter peanuts everywhere.

John returned with the drink, either not noticing or choosing to ignore the mess. "Here you are," he said, placing the glass on Cini's tray.

"Where are the washrooms?" Cini asked abruptly.

John pointed to a door just a few feet ahead in the front of first class. "Just here, sir."

"It's occupied," Cini stated, though he hadn't moved to check.

John, looking puzzled, opened the door to reveal an empty lavatory. "No sir, it isn't."

"There's another one, isn't there?" Cini pressed.

"Well yes, just ahead of the curtains - in the lounge," John answered, a hint of confusion in his voice.

Without another word, Cini downed his Screwdriver in one gulp, stood up, and headed for the lounge washroom.

As the lavatory door clicked shut behind Cini, a sense of unease settled over the first-class cabin. The other passengers exchanged glances, their earlier curiosity about the man in the oversized coat now tinged with concern.

John and Mary shared a look of their own, a silent communication born of years working together. Something was off about this passenger, but neither could have imagined the terror that was about to unfold.

In the cramped confines of the airplane bathroom, Cini started peeling the silver duct tape off the shopping bag, his heart pounding in his chest. He closed his eyes, taking deep breaths to steady himself. The moment he had been planning for was finally here. As he prepared to set his plan in motion, the lives of everyone on Flight 812 hung in the balance, blissfully unaware of the danger that had boarded the plane with them.

Chapter 8: The Hijacking

The night sky stretched endlessly above Flight 812, a tapestry of stars punctuated by a sliver of crescent moon. Inside the plane, however, an altogether different kind of darkness was about to descend.

John was preparing the hot hors d'oeuvres service for the first-class passengers in the galley. As he worked, he glanced at his watch, then back to Cini's empty seat. The peculiar passenger who had retreated to the lounge washroom had been gone for an unusually long time. As he went back into the cabin to pick up empty glasses and discarded napkins, a nagging sense of unease tugged at John's mind.

A lady in 4D, her silver hair neatly coiffed, caught John's attention. "Could I trouble you for a gin and tonic dear?" she asked with a smile.

"Of course, ma'am," John replied, his professional demeanor masking his growing concern. He made his way back to the galley, reaching for a bottle of Gordon's gin. Just as his fingers closed around the cool glass, a voice behind him made his blood run cold.

"Over here."

John turned slowly, his heart hammering in his chest. There, in the first row of the empty lounge, sat the man from 2B. But he was transformed, a nightmare come to life. A black balaclava covered his face. Atop the balaclava sat a curly black wig, adding to his menacing appearance. But it was what he held in his hands that made John's breath catch in his throat: a double-barreled 12-gauge sawed-off shotgun, pointing directly at John's head.

"Where the hell did you come from?" John managed to choke out, his voice barely above a whisper.

"Get over here and sit down!" Cini barked, his voice muffled but menacing behind the mask.

John's instincts screamed at him to run, to call for help, but the reality of the situation kept him rooted to the spot. "You're kidding!" he said, a desperate attempt to deny the horror unfolding before him.

"When I blow your head through the fucking side of the plane, you'll know I'm not kidding." Cini's response chilled him to the bone.

With no choice, John complied, taking a seat in the centre of the row facing Cini. A small table separated them, but the distance felt nonexistent with the shotgun trained on him. Cini produced a folded yellow paper, thrusting it towards John.

"Don't you look at that," he snapped as John began to unfold it. "I want you to take it to the Captain - and tell him to follow the instructions to a 'T'."

Before John could respond, Mary walked into the lounge, her voice chipper and oblivious to the danger. "John, I need help with some extra wine glasses. There's not enough..."

Her words trailed off as she took in the scene before her. The hooded figure turned towards her, his voice low and threatening. "Sit down."

Mary stood frozen, her eyes wide with disbelief and fear.

"Sit. Down." The man repeated, each word dripping with menace.

John's voice was barely audible. "Sit down, Mary. It's for real."

As Mary sank into the seat beside John, the hijacker pressed the barrels of his gun against her forehead. The cold metal sent shivers down her spine.

"Don't be long," he growled at John, "or I'll blow her head off. And don't make any plans up there."

With trembling hands, John took the note and made his way to the cockpit. As the door closed behind him, the sky pirate turned his attention back to Mary.

"Don't sit there," he commanded. "Get over there, by the window. Put your back up against it and stare straight ahead. If you turn your head, I'll blow it off."

Mary complied, her movements mechanical, as if she were sleepwalking through a terrible dream. She pressed her back against the cool window, her eyes fixed on the small window in the entrance door across the aisle. The gun remained trained on her head as Cini fumbled a smoke into his mouth one-handed from a soft pack of Winstons, lighting up with a Zippo lighter. The acrid smell of cigarette smoke and lighter fluid filled the air.

In the cockpit, John's whispered words sent a chill through the air. "Captain, there's a man back there with a gun."

Captain Ehman's skeptical look quickly faded as he saw the terror in John's eyes. "For real?"

"It's for real," John confirmed. "He wants me to give you this note."

Captain Ehman unfolded the yellow paper and began to read the note aloud. It was riddled with typos and broken English.

"I do not want the news to hear of this till we have picked up our cargo.
Captain, if I see anyone come out of the flight deck they will be minus a head.
I have, just boarded your plane with 54 sticks of dynamite (60 per cent each) and one shotgun and lots of shells, this being my last note I want to make it long. If everyone stays away from me no harm will come to them or the plan, anyone on or off this plane makes a move I don't like it will only mean that they will make heaven before the rest of us.
Just keep this in mind if the Lord did not want this, I would not be

The cockpit fell silent as the gravity of the situation became a
horrifying reality.

Back in the lounge, Mary remained motionless, her eyes fixed straight
ahead. A movement in her peripheral vision caught her attention - Al

Solosky, a first-class passenger returning from the washroom. Their eyes met for a brief, terrifying moment. Mary's gaze flickered, a silent warning. Solosky, taking in the scene, quietly retreated to his seat, the weight of what he'd witnessed heavy on his shoulders.

John returned, resuming his seat beside Mary. The hijacker's voice cut through the tense silence. "Did the Captain get the message?"

"Yes."

"So he understands I want 1.5 million dollars waiting for us in Great Falls?"

"Yes."

A long, awkward silence stretched between them, broken only by the steady hum of the engines and Cini's rhythmic drags on his cigarette.

"Good," the man finally said, the single word hanging in the air heavy with menace.

As the reality of their situation sank in, Mary and John exchanged a glance. In that moment, they both knew that the routine flight they had embarked on earlier that day had transformed into a nightmare at 37,000 feet. The original Doomsday Flight had begun. The fate of everyone on board now rested in their hands, and in the unpredictable whims of a madman with a gun.

Chapter 9: Tension and Revelations

The night sky stretched endlessly beyond the windows of Flight 812, the vastness of space a stark contrast to the claustrophobic tension within the aircraft. In the cockpit, Captain Ehman's voice, steady despite the circumstances, broke the eerie quiet.

"Mayday, Mayday, Mayday. ATC Winnipeg, this is Air Canada 812. Be advised that we are being hijacked. I repeat, we are being hijacked. We have been directed to proceed to Great Falls, Montana. Please advise. Over."

After what felt like an eternity, ATC Winnipeg's response crackled through the radio. "Roger Air Canada 812. Understood. Stand by for new heading."

In the lounge, Cini's agitation grew as the plane maintained its course. "We haven't changed course," he snapped at John. "Go back and see that they understand."

As John headed back to the cockpit, Cini turned his attention to Mary. From his package, he produced two wires, his masked face unreadable as he stared at her. "Come over here," he commanded.

Mary's heart raced, but she kept her voice steady. "You mean you want me to get up and sit down beside you?"

"Yes."

As Mary complied, Cini's voice took on an almost apologetic tone. "Lady, I don't want to frighten you."

"I know, dear," Mary replied, her voice gentle despite her fear.

Cini handed her the two wires. "OK, now hold these wires apart in your left hand." As Mary positioned the wires, wedging one in the crook of her thumb and forefinger and one next to her pinky, Cini's next words sent a chill through her. "If you want to die, put the wires together. If you don't, keep them apart."

The weight of their predicament settled heavily on Mary as she held the wires, acutely aware that her life—and potentially the lives of everyone on board—now literally rested in her hands.

Back in the cockpit, John relayed the message from Cini. "Captain. He wants to know if you understand him. He's frustrated that we haven't changed course yet."

"Tell him that we fully understand his demands and we are currently calculating our course to Great Falls. We have requested headings from air traffic control." The captain explained. "We'll be heading there as soon as humanly possible." He shook his head. "Jesus, what a nightmare. How are the rest of the passengers and crew?"

"Only Mary is with us." John explained. "None of the other passengers and crew know what's happening."

"OK, stay calm and level-headed." The captain encouraged. "We'll get through this. Just placate this guy as best you can."

"Yessir."

No sooner had John sat back down in the lounge when the plane started banking right towards Montana. The change in course seemed to calm Cini. This momentary relief was shattered by a deafening blast when, without warning, he discharged his shotgun.

The deafening blast shook the plane. Shards of fiberglass and debris from the bulkhead separating the lounge and the cockpit swirled around the pilots.

"Oxygen!" yelled the captain.

They scrambled to don oxygen masks, fearing a breach in the fuselage. Captain Ehman's steady hand on the control column guided the plane into a descent as they assessed the damage.

"Pressure reading!?!"

"Pressure's normal." Second Officer Belanger replied through the mask's mic. "I don't think the fuselage has been breached."

John burst back into the cockpit. "Captain. He accidentally discharged his shotgun. No one is hurt."

As the immediate crisis passed, the crew removed their masks, their faces etched with the strain of the situation.

"Thank God." Captain Ehman sighed with relief. "Do whatever he tells you. Also ask him who we're to get this money from." He pulled back on the yolk and pushed the autopilot button once again."

In the lounge, Cini's panic was evident even behind his mask. He turned to Mary stammering, "I'm sorry, I didn't mean to do that."

Mary, her nurturing instincts kicking in once again despite her fear, spoke soothingly. "I know you didn't, dear. Would you like me to hold your hand?"

As Cini replaced the shotgun shell, he nodded, allowing Mary to take his hand. Her right hand clasped his, while her left continued its crucial task of keeping the wires apart. The simple human contact seemed to calm him slightly. John sat back down.

"So the cockpit understands what has to happen?" inquired Cini.

"They understand." Replied John. "We're to go to Montana, pick up the money, then go to Regina, release the passengers, load the aircraft full of guns and ammunition and head for Ireland. Right?"

"Right."

"There's just one thing." John continued. "The captain wants to know just who we are to get the money from."

"Air Canada supplies the money." Cini responded

"OK." John returned to the cockpit.

An unexpected connection was forming between captor and hostage. Mary introduced herself to Cini. "My name is Mary. Please call me Mary."

"Mary," Cini repeated. "That's a nice name." A hint of warmth in his voice.

"Oh, do you really like it?" Mary asked, seizing on this moment of connection.

"Yes."

"And what's your name, dear?"

"Dennis."

"May I call you Dennis?"

As Cini nodded, John returned from the cockpit. Mary, taking the opportunity to further disarm their hijacker, announced, "His name is Dennis."

"Well then, Dennis," John replied "may I tell the passengers what the blast was about? The crew in economy's been calling the captain about it."

"Tell them a light bulb blew."

"But Dennis, sir, I…" John is cut off by Cini screaming in his face.

The conversation that followed revealed the depths of Cini's paranoia and instability.

"Sir? SIR?!" shouted Cini. "I knew it. You're FBI or RCMP aren't you? They all say "sir". And I'm going to kill them all. All the FBI that come to the airport in Great Falls. And all the RCMP in Regina. And you're one of them."

"No sir…I mean Dennis. I'm not a policeman. I'm a purser." John clarified.

"What nationality are you?" inquired Cini.

"French Canadian"

Cini calmed down. "OK. You're safe. But I'll kill every Englishman on this flight."

John sat quietly.

Cini contemplated. "Don't worry. I like you. I won't kill you." He turned 180 degrees, "When I get the money and we land in Ireland I'll take care of you. You won't have to work for a long time." He tilted his head towards the aft. "Now go and tell the passengers whatever you like. Get back here after you're done."

John headed back into first-class.

"Ladies and gentleman, may I have your attention please. We are currently being hijacked." John announced calmly.

Two of the passengers got up and ran back into economy.

"and it's very important" he continued "that you don't tell him you're English."

"But I am English." The man in 3B declared.

"Well don't tell him or he'll shoot you." John warned. 3B nodded with purpose.

"Now, who wants a drink?" John asked. Every hand went up.

Back in the cockpit Captain Ehman was on the radio with Air Canada HQ.

"Please be advised that we have instructions that we can't land in Great Falls until the money is ready." The captain explained. "It also has to be delivered by a woman. We'll do a very slow bank around Great Falls until you've got it together. We've got fuel for another 2 and a half hours. Over."

"Air Canada 812, we're making all the necessary arrangements." HQ responded. "Will advise when we're ready for you in Great Falls. Over."

"Roger that."

In the lounge Mary continued her efforts to connect with Cini.

"You know Mary. I have a mission," he explained. "I have to help the Irish."

"Oh Dennis. I'm Irish," Mary replied.

"You are?" Cini said surprisingly. "Well that's good"

"Do you have any family?" she asked gently.

"No, not anymore," Cini replied, his voice tinged with sadness.

"Tell me, what's your story, Dennis? Where are you from?"

"That's not important right now," Cini deflected. "Besides, there's not much to tell. I want to hear about you, Mary. Where did you grow up?"

"Well, I don't really like to talk about it." Mary said reluctantly.

"I insist." Persisted Cini. "We have all the time in the world."

Mary began to share her story. "Well, I was the youngest of 14 if you can believe it. We all lived in a little 2-story house in St. Bride's Newfoundland. When I was just 3, my mother passed. Well this was just too much for my father to handle. It was the middle of the depression you see. So he decided to put my brother Jack and I up for foster care. I do think it was with a heavy heart but he didn't have much choice back then."

Cini listened intently and squeezed Mary's hand tighter.

She wiped back tears. "My foster parents were awful. I can remember I was 5-years-old and my foster mother would bark at me... "You're no good, you'll end up down in a gutter." Until I was 8 I never once saw the inside of a school. I had one dress which was never washed. I was treated like Cinderella. Basically a slave to them. They made me get down on my knees and scrub the floor. I was regularly beaten with a belt and my foster mother would always tell her husband "make sure there's a buckle on it". I was lucky to get a crust of bread to eat, even if it was moldy."

Mary continued. "I was sent barefoot into town to do errands and I would eat berries and what fruit I could find along the way. I learned to raid all the best gardens in town. They never made a fence I couldn't jump." She chuckled. "I'd eat carrots without even washing them off."

As Mary recounted her harrowing childhood experiences - the neglect, the abuse, the hunger - Cini's grip on her hand tightened. His body language shifted, the menacing terrorist giving way to a man moved by another's suffering.

"Oh wow. I'm really sorry you had to go through that, Mary," Cini said, his voice thick with emotion.

Mary continued her story, detailing how she ended up in an orphanage in St. John's and her eventual adoption at the age of 10. This is when her life started to finally change for the better her adopted parents loving and supportive. After high school she started down the path that led her to become a stewardess.

"You see Dennis. In those days it was a prerequisite to have a nurse's diploma in order to become a stewardess." As she spoke, her mind drifted back to a pivotal moment in her journey - her training as a psychiatric nurse in St. John's Hospital in the autumn of 1955.

The memory surfaced vividly, as if it had happened yesterday instead of over a decade ago....

Mary, then a young psychiatric nurse student, walked nervously down a dimly lit hallway alongside Dr. Henry Kim, a respected professor and psychiatrist, his presence both reassuring and intimidating. Her clipboard clutched tightly to her chest, she checked her watch anxiously.

"Jim has been very agitated lately, Mary," Dr. Kim explained in a low voice. "Just stay calm and follow my lead."

Mary nodded, her nervousness constrained by curiosity and determination. They stopped at a door labeled "Patient Room 213."

As Dr. Kim unlocked the door, he called out, "Jim, it's Dr. Kim. I'm here to say hello with my friend Mary."

Taking a deep breath, Mary followed Dr. Kim into the room. Inside, a man paced back and forth, muttering to himself and occasionally shouting incomprehensible words. Mary hesitated, intimidated by the raw energy emanating from the patient.

Jim noticed her and immediately stopped pacing, his wild eyes fixing on her with an intensity that made her want to step back. But Mary stood her ground, remembering her training.

"Jim, this is Mary," Dr. Kim said calmly. "She's a student I'm working with. We're here to see how you're doing."

Summoning her courage, Mary spoke keeping her voice calm and steady… "Hi Jim. I'm Mary. I'm a new student here at the hospital. How are you feeling today?"

Jim didn't respond, his gaze darting between Mary and Dr. Kim., his breathing heavy and erratic.

"We're here to check on you and see if there's anything you need," said Dr. Kim in a hushed tone. "Would you like to talk about how you're feeling?"

Suddenly, without warning, Jim lunged at Mary, grabbing her clipboard and pen and throwing them across the room.

"You don't know me!" he shouted, his face contorted with anger and fear. "Nobody knows me! They all think I'm crazy, but I'm not! You can't keep me here!"

Mary's heart raced, but she forced herself to remain calm. "Jim, I understand that you're feeling upset right now," she said softly. "Can you tell me more about what's bothering you?"

Jim paused, looking at her with suspicion. "You're just like all the others. You don't care about me. You're here to keep me locked up."

In that moment, Mary felt a connection to Jim's pain. She remembered her own feelings of helplessness and fear from her childhood. "I hear you, Jim," she said, her voice gentle but firm. "It can be scary to be in a place like this, but I promise you that we're here to help you. Would you like to take a deep breath with me?"

She held out her hands, and after a moment's hesitation, Jim took them. Mary closed her eyes and took a deep breath, guiding Jim to do the same. Slowly, she led them to sit on the bed.

"Let's talk about you," Mary whispered. "I want to know everything you're struggling with. Let's work through it together, Jim."

Jim's anger crumbled, replaced by heart-wrenching sobs. Mary hugged him, patting his back comfortingly. "It's hard," he choked out. "The pain is real."

"I know, Jim," Mary replied, her own eyes misting over. "Believe me, I do."

As the memory faded, Mary found herself back in the present, still holding Cini's hand on the hijacked plane, still keeping the wires apart with her other. She realized that the skills she had learned as a psychiatric nurse - the ability to remain calm in the face of volatility, to connect with people in distress - were serving her well in this crisis. She looked at Cini - or Dennis, as she now knew him - and saw not just a dangerous hijacker, but a troubled soul in pain.

"After my time training as a nurse," Mary continued, her voice soft but steady, "I became an airline stewardess. I wanted to see the world, to experience life beyond the confines of my difficult childhood. But I've never forgotten the lessons I've learned over the years - about compassion, about understanding, about the power of human connection."

Little did Cini know that Mary had trained as a psychiatric nurse. The skills she learned very much coming into play as she slowly but surely gained his trust. Her tale of resilience, of overcoming a painful past to become the woman she was today, seemed to touch something in him.

Cini listened intently, his grip on the shotgun loosening slightly. "You've been through so much, Mary," he said, his voice tinged with a mix of admiration and shame. "And here you are, still trying to help others. Even me." A fragile connection was forming between captor and hostage.

Mary squeezed his hand gently. "We all have our struggles, Dennis. Sometimes, what we need most is someone to listen, to understand. I'm here to listen if you want to talk."

"You're a kind woman, Mary," Cini whispered. "Even after all you've been through. I'm going to help some people as well. I have a mission. I have to help the Irish Republican Army. They need me. I went to chapel this morning and prayed about it."

The air in the lounge, so recently filled with fear and tension, now hummed with a complex mix of emotions—empathy, sorrow, and the faintest glimmer of hope. As Flight 812 continued its journey towards an uncertain fate, the human drama unfolding served as a poignant reminder of the power of compassion and the unpredictable nature of human connections, even in the most dire of circumstances.

Chapter 10: Escalation

The brief serene atmosphere in the lounge was shattered when Phillip Bonne, the 22-year-old assistant purser in charge of economy class, walked in unknowingly. Cini's reaction was immediate and violent.

"Sit down!" he barked, pointing his shotgun at the startled young man.

Phillip, his eyes wide with shock, quickly complied, taking a seat next to John. Cini's paranoia surged to the forefront once more.

"What nationality are you?" he demanded.

"French Canadian," Phillip replied, his voice trembling slightly.

Cini's response was chilling. "I'll blow your head off. The FLQ would be proud of me and De Gaulle would turn over in his grave."

The three crew members exchanged nervous glances, not quite understanding the twisted logic behind Cini's threat. Before they could process it, Cini barked another order.

"Get up and pull the curtains shut between economy and first class."

As Phillip moved to obey, Mary's gentle voice cut through the tension. "Why should he do that, Dennis?"

In response, Cini pulled out two bundles of dynamite from his coat pocket, each containing five sticks with fuses protruding from the ends. "Because I'm going to light one of these and throw it inside," he stated matter-of-factly.

Mary's heart raced, but she maintained her composure. "Oh Dennis. Why would you do that, dear? You're going to hurt all those people. Do you know those people, Dennis?"

"No," Cini replied after a moment's hesitation. His resolve seemed to waver, "Call him back."

"Phillip come back!" Mary screamed. He swiftly returned and Cini ordered him to sit down.

"I'm hot under the hood," he proclaimed. The wool balaclava was doing its job. Cini turned to John. "Turn down the temperature." John went to the thermostat panel and lowered it from 70 to 55. Within a few minutes the lounge grew cold.

"I'm freezing," Mary said to Cini. "Can I please get a sweater?" Cini looked at Phillip. "Get her a sweater." Phillip returned quickly with her sweater. Cini took the wires from Mary's left hand for a moment as she put it on.

"Give me a Kleenex," Cini ordered. Phillip handed him one, and he wiped his eyes as he whimpered quietly.

"Could I put on my jacket please?" John asked. Cini nodded. As John slid the jacket on, Cini noticed the single gold braid wrapped around each sleeve and started to yell.

"Now I KNOW you're the FBI!"

What happened next seemed to unfold in slow motion. Cini grabbed a stick of dynamite, shoved it into John's mouth and pressed his shotgun against his temple.

"NOW! Move your head toward the hole!" He pointed toward the shattered section of the cockpit wall. "I'll show you just how big a hole I can make!" John leaned his head back but gently pushed the barrel of the gun away from his head.

"Dennis, dear," Mary pleaded, "why don't you put the safety catch on the gun?"

He turned to Mary. "You. Lean over the table." He took the wires from her hand. "Take her hands," he said to Phillip.

Mary and Phillip grasped hands across the table between them.

"I want to see the whites of your knuckles," Cini asserted.

"Dennis, you don't want to hurt us do you dear?" Mary implored. Her voice remained steady, though her hands trembled in Phillip's grip. She was counting on the connection she'd built with Cini, the trust she'd carefully cultivated. Cini was panting under his breath. John sat quietly with the dynamite still in his mouth.

As the situation in the lounge grew increasingly volatile, events were unfolding rapidly elsewhere.

The November night hung cold and clear over Mountain Home US Air Force Base, the sprawling military installation nestled in the rugged terrain of southwestern Idaho. Inside the base cafeteria, the fluorescent lights hummed steadily over about two dozen Air Force personnel as they settled into their evening routine, the clatter of metal utensils against plastic trays providing a familiar backdrop to their casual conversations.

The evening's comfortable monotony was quickly shattered. The base-wide speaker system squealed to life, and a sharp, authoritative voice cut through the ambient chatter:

"SCRAMBLE, SCRAMBLE, SCRAMBLE, SCRAMBLE!"

In an instant, the base erupted into action. Air personnel rushed from the cafeteria to their stations, and in the hangar, crews hurriedly prepared two USAF McDonnell F-101 Voodoo jet fighters for takeoff. The screech of metal against concrete echoed through the space as wheel chocks were yanked away from the landing gear. Engine covers were stripped off with practiced movements, exposing the powerful Pratt & Whitney J57 turbojets that would soon roar to life.

Two aluminum maintenance ladders were rolled into position beside each aircraft. The four crew members—two pilots and two radar intercept officers—were already approaching in their flight gear, their movements quick but measured. They climbed into their respective cockpits with the fluid efficiency that came from countless drills. Outside, the Idaho night was peaceful for just a moment longer. Then the runway erupted with activity as the two Voodoos taxied into position. Their powerful engines spooled up, the whine building to a crescendo before the afterburners kicked in with a thunderous roar. Brilliant blue-white flames shot from the exhaust nozzles, painting the darkness with stark, artificial daylight.

The first Voodoo accelerated down the runway, its landing lights cutting through the darkness like spears. As it lifted off, the second fighter followed in perfect staggered formation, their afterburners leaving trails of fire against the star-studded Idaho sky. Within moments, both aircraft had vanished into the night, leaving only their fading engine noise and the lingering smell of jet fuel as evidence of their passage as they streaked towards their intercept point; Air Canada Flight 812.

Back on the DC-8, the tension continued to mount. Cini's erratic behavior was keeping everyone on edge.

John reached up and slowly removed the stick of dynamite from his mouth.

"Who told you to take that out?" Cini shouted. He ripped it out of John's hand and shoved it back in his mouth. Then, in an instant, ripped it back out of John's mouth and handed it to Mary.

"Smell that!" he exclaimed.

Mary retorted, "My darling, I don't know anything about dynamite."

"I didn't think you did." He replied as he laid the stick on the table. He turned to John.

"What's taking so long?"

"We can't land the plane until we have the money in hand. You insisted on that. Remember?" he reminded the madman, "It's hard to raise 1.5 million dollars in cash on a Sunday with all the banks closed."

"Right," Cini replied.

He pulled a small transistor radio from his coat pocket and turned it on. "If I hear anything about this hijacking, you're all dead." He clicked it on and slowly rotated the tuner dial but only gets static and crackling music so he shut it off.

Suddenly he turned to Mary. "You want to be the stewardess of the year?"

"Why Dennis? What do you want me to do?" she asked.

He held up the shotgun. "I want you to take this and shoot me."

"Oh Dennis. Why would I want to hurt you, dear? You're not going to hurt us," Mary said, her voice steady and soothing.

"How do you know?" Cini challenged.

"Because you told me and I believe you," she said.

Cini thrust the gun toward John with trembling hands. "Shoot me," he demanded, his voice raw with desperation.

"I can't, Dennis," John replied, his face pale with tension.

"Why?" Cini's eyes narrowed. "Haven't you killed anybody before?"

"No, I haven't." John's voice was barely above a whisper.

Cini waved the gun in John's face, the metal catching the light as it moved. "Well, if you don't kill me, I'll shoot you."

Standing his ground despite the weapon inches from his face, John's response was steady. "Then you'll have to because I can't kill anybody."

Cini studied him for a moment before nodding slowly. "Good," he said, lowering the weapon. "You're a lucky man. If you'd grabbed for the gun, I'd have put the wires together." He gestured toward the front of the aircraft. "Go ask the captain what's happening."

John rose from his seat, his legs slightly unsteady, and headed into the cockpit.

"He wants to know what's happening," he announced as he entered the flight deck.

Captain Ehman kept his eyes fixed on the instruments as he responded. "We're still waiting for instructions to land. We just talked to Air Canada headquarters. The president says that the money is on the way." He paused, then added firmly, "Also let him know there will be no FBI on the tarmac at Great Falls."

When John returned to the lounge, Cini was waiting expectantly. "They're still waiting for delivery of the money. Once it's there we'll get instructions to land."

"Fine." Cini's eyes narrowed suspiciously. "How will I know there'll be no FBI guys waiting?"

"Because the President has promised us."

"What President?"

"The President of the United States."

"Good." He turned his attention to Mary, his demeanor suddenly shifting. "You know what? I've got a king-sized hangover."

"Why dear?" Mary asked, her voice gentle despite the circumstances.

"Because I haven't eaten in two days and I've been drinking."

"Why were you drinking?"

Cini sounded shameful. "To get up enough nerve to do this. I was going to hijack another flight yesterday but I backed down at the last minute."

The radio crackled to life in the headsets in the cockpit. "Okay Air Canada 812, we've got the money ready," came the voice from Great Falls Air Traffic Control. "You're cleared to land on runway 21."

"Copy that Great Falls. Air Canada 812 cleared to land on runway 21," Captain Ehman responded, already beginning to angle the nose of the plane downward toward Great Falls airport.

Back in the lounge, Cini turned to Mary once more. "Alright, I think we're landing," he said, his voice tight with nervous energy. "Go up front and tell them that when we land in Great Falls they're to go to the end of the runway and get ready for immediate takeoff. But tell them to go past the terminal building first so I can see the Great Falls sign."

"OK Dennis," Mary replied unclasping Phillips hands and rising from her seat.

When she reached the cockpit, she delivered the message. "Captain. He wants to see the Great Falls sign."

Captain Ehman nodded grimly. "Just tell him to keep those damn wires apart."

"It's okay, Vern," Mary assured him. "I'm sitting beside him."

As the plane began its descent towards Great Falls, Cini's agitation grew. He placed his two bundles of dynamite on the table before him, positioning the fuses to face his direction. With practiced movements, he pulled out his Zippo lighter, its unusually long four-inch flame dancing as he waved it menacingly back and forth in front of the fuses.

Mary had just settled back into her seat beside him when the plane's wheels met the runway with a firm thud. Cini extinguished the lighter and handed Mary the wires. She took it in her left hand and Cini pressed the cold steel of the shotgun barrels against her temple.

Outside, under the cover of darkness, the Air Canada DC-8 made its way slowly past the terminal building of Great Falls International Airport. Despite the president's assurances, FBI agents lined the runway, their presence a clear violation of the agreement.

"Air Canada 812, the FBI is asking if they should intervene," ground control inquired.

"No way! Stand down!" Captain Ehman barked into his headset, his voice sharp with urgency.

The massive aircraft came to a stop at the end of the taxiway. Fuel trucks converged on the plane. Through the cockpit window, they could see a black unmarked police cruiser approach and stop about two hundred feet from the nose of the aircraft. A young female police officer emerged, clutching a briefcase and walked toward the plane. Captain Ehman caught sight of her and waved her toward the front entrance door before heading back to the lounge.

"The briefcase full of money is ready," he announced before heading back into the cockpit.

Cini's eyes narrowed. "Tie it onto something and bring it in."

"There's an emergency strap in the cockpit that would probably work," Phillip suggested.

"Fine. Go get it."

Phillip retrieved the emergency escape strap from the cockpit, cutting a long length before returning to the exit door.

"Don't open the door more than 6 inches," Cini warned, his voice tight with tension.

Phillip eased the door open just enough to lower the strap to the waiting officer. She secured the briefcase, and he began to pull it up, only to discover a problem – the case wouldn't fit through the narrow opening.

"Dennis," John said carefully, "it won't fit through the crack in the door. Plus we'll need to open the door all the way in order to close it."

"I don't care how you get the money in here," Cini snapped. "Just don't open that door any wider. And go tell the Captain he has 15 minutes to refuel."

As John departed for the cockpit, Mary exchanged a meaningful glance with Phillip. In a moment of quick thinking, Mary created a distraction. She held out the wires toward Cini. "Dennis, will you please hold this for a minute while I blow my nose?"

The moment Cini turned to look at Mary, Phillip seized his chance. In one swift motion, he yanked the door wide open, hauled the briefcase inside, and slammed it shut. The sound made Cini whirl back around.

"Did you get it?" he demanded.

"Yes," Phillip answered, untying the briefcase and passing it to Cini.

Cini flipped the lid open briefly, his eyes widening at the sight of the thick bundles of cash packed inside. The crew exchanged glances. They had successfully delivered the ransom, but they knew this was far from over. The real challenge lay ahead: how to end this hijacking without loss of life.

With the money now in his possession, Cini's unpredictable nature became even more dangerous. As Flight 812 prepared for takeoff once more, the crew knew they were embarking on the most perilous leg of their journey yet.

Chapter 11: Race Against Time

"Count the money." Cini tossed the case to John.

John settled across the table from Cini and Mary, opening the briefcase with steady hands despite his racing heart. Each bundle was wrapped with strips marked "$10,000." He pulled out his pen from his breast pocket, grabbed a sickness bag from the side pocket, and began the count.

He pulled a bundle of cash out and slipped off the strip. He undid the elastic band that's wrapped underneath. The first bundle revealed the deception – after the initial $100 bill, the rest were fives. John maintained his poker face, methodically thumbing through the cash bill by bill. He quickly finishes "counting" the bills in the bundle. He snaps the elastic band back on, slips on the strip of paper and sets it aside on the table. He writes down "10,000" on the barf bag.

After about 20 bundles are neatly stacked beside the briefcase Cini interrupted John's counting and motioned him toward the cockpit. "Okay. We take off now."

John stopped counting and headed back into the cockpit. "He wants to go right now," he said to to the crew. "Okay" responded Captain Ehman. He put his headset back on. "Great Falls Air Canada 812 ready for takeoff."

"Roger Air Canada 812 cleared for immediate takeoff runway 03."

"Air Canada 812 cleared for takeoff runway 03." Ehman responded.

Ehman moved the throttle up slightly and lumbered the DC-8 toward the runway.

After lining up on 03 it was full throttle and the DC-8 took off into the Montana night sky.

John finished counting and placed the last bundle onto a neat stack on the table. According to the chicken scratch on the barf bag there was $1.5 million.

"How much is there?" Cini asked.

"Exactly one and a half million."

Cini's command was predictable: "Count it again."

John glances at Mary briefly with disdain and starts the process over again.

Outside, the two F-101 Voodoos approached through the night sky. "Reaper 1 to Mountain Home tower, we have a visual on the target," the lead pilot reported, his voice breaking through the static.

"Copy that Reaper 1," replied the Air Force General back at Mountain Home. "Stand off and maintain visual contact."

John finished counting the last of the bills for the second time, replaced the elastic band and slips the $10,000 paper slip back on. He placed it with the other bundles back into the briefcase.

"How much?" Cini asked.

"A million and a half."

John tried to diffuse the tension with gallows humour. Tossing his tie across the bundles of money, he quipped, "Old tie... you've never been closer to so much money in your life."

Cini's hysterical laughter filled the lounge, a sound that sent chills down Mary's spine. As John joined in the laughter, perhaps from relief, perhaps from hysteria, Mary closed her eyes and began to pray under her breath.

"Lord, please don't let me die in vain. I don't want to. Let me help. First save the passengers, dear Lord. And then save the crew." She looked up at Cini who's still chuckling.

Drawing on her training once more, Mary saw an opening. "Oh Dennis, I can hear the children crying."

The effect was immediate. "What? There are kids on this flight?"

"Yes, Dennis. The dear little souls are so tired and hungry. They don't even know what's going on."

Mary watched as compassion flickered across what little she could see of Cini's face behind the balaclava. Her gambit worked. Cini turned to John.

"Turn this airplane around. We're going back to Great Falls. I want the passengers to get off."

"All the passengers?" John inquired.

"Yes," Cini responded. "I also want a full load of fuel."

"OK. What about the crew?"

"The crew at the back can go."

John got up. "I'll let the Captain know."

He opened the cockpit door just as Captain Ehman was signing off from Great Falls ATC.

"Appreciate your help Great Falls. Air Canada 812 out."

John piped up, "So he wants you to go back to Great Falls and let the passengers off."

"Seriously?" Ehman said with a hint of rhetoric.

"He's dead serious. He also wants to fill up on fuel."

The Captain let out a heavy sigh and pressed a button on the yoke. "Great Falls Air Canada 812 there's been a change of plans. Sorry fellas. We're coming back in to drop the passengers off. I want buses for the passengers, trucks for the baggage and a full load of fuel."

"Roger Air Canada 812 we'll be ready for you. Cleared for landing runway 21."

As they began their descent back to Great Falls, Cini pulled out a baggage claim ticket and handed it to John. "I've got a blue suitcase on board. Everything I own is in it. When we land, I'll give you ten minutes to get it. Understand?"

John nodded. "OK"

The DC-8 touched down and started taxiing to the waiting buses and fuel trucks at the end of the runway when an unfamiliar voice came through the cockpit crew's headset.

"Captain Ehman this is FBI Special Agent Gary Carter. Do you read me?"

"Loud and clear."

The agent continued, "I'm tasked with handling this situation and we have a number of SWAT team members at hand ready and waiting. Do you want any help?"

"No thank you," replied Ehman in a hushed voice. "I'm afraid if he sees one of you guys he'll blow us all up."

"OK...we're here if you need us."

"Thank you. But please keep your men out of sight," the captain implored. "This guy's really anxious and has a lot of fire power onboard."

"Got it."

As the plane came to a stop at the end of the runway, John got up.

"You've got 10 minutes," Cini snapped. "If you're not back with my suitcase, I'll blow Mary's head off." The gravity of the situation suddenly became clear.

John glanced at his watch - 9:02 - nodded and headed to the exit door. Just as he started opening it a stair truck hit it.

"Back up dammit!" he yelled. "Back up!" The truck driver threw it in reverse and backs away briefly while John swung the door all the way open. He directed the truck back in and ran down the stairs to where a belt loader was just pulling up to the open baggage hold.

"Who's in charge here?" John demanded.

A husky man wearing an orange safety vest piped up, "I'm Ground Supervisor."

John hands him Cini's baggage slip. "Here. Find this suitcase. It's blue and it's critical that we find it ASAP. Lives are at stake."

The Supe glances at the tag. "Alright. Heads up people! We're looking for a blue suitcase. Baggage tag ending in 150. Time is of the essence."

John and the ground personnel get to work.

Back in the lounge Cini still has the gun on Mary's temple.

"Do you think they'll try anything?" he asked Mary uneasily.

"No, they won't dear. Don't worry." Mary replied calmly

"They better not." Cini growled as he glanced at his watch.

Meanwhile John frantically rummaged through the bags in the hold.
He finally came across a navy blue suitcase. He looks at the tag.
605150.

"Bingo" John muttered under his breath. He looked at his watch –
9:13.

"Fuck!"

He lugged it out from deep in the hold and hustled down the belt
loader.

He started for the steps with the bag and almost collapsed. The suitcase
is extremely heavy.

"What the hell has he got in here?" he thought to himself.

Inside the plane, Mary faced what could have been her final moments
as Cini watched the time tick past the deadline.

"I'm sorry I have to kill you, Mary. I'm a man of my word."

Mary's voice remained steady, though her heart pounded. "May I turn
and look at you, dear?"

"Go ahead."

As she turned to face the shotgun barrels with Cini's finger on the
trigger, Mary drew upon every ounce of her training and life
experience. "Dennis. Do you actually want to kill me?"

"No."

She placed a gentle hand on his knee, just as she had done with
countless troubled patients before. "Well then, dear, will you please
wait just a little longer? John will be back with your suitcase. It's dark
outside and he's looking for a suitcase he's never seen."

John lumbered up the stairs as passengers are coming down. At the top someone grabbed his hand helping him into the plane where dozens of passengers are crammed in the aisle. He got more than a few pats on the back and words of encouragement.

The seconds stretched like hours until John finally burst into the lounge, dragging the heavy suitcase. Mary's whispered "Thank you God" spoke for everyone in the room.

The weight of the suitcase wasn't lost on John – whatever Cini had packed for his escape seemed far heavier than normal luggage. But for now, they had survived another crisis point, though Mary knew from the look in Cini's eyes that the most dangerous part of their ordeal still lay ahead.

Chapter 12: The Last Passengers

After the last passenger filed out of the aircraft, Phillip returned to the lounge to report. Cini's paranoia surfaced immediately.

"I hope nobody's trying to get on here." his voice tight with suspicion.

"They're not."

"Go and check again."

As Phillip left to double-check the cabin, Cini leaned close to Mary, his voice dropping to a whisper. "Do you want to get off too?"

Mary recognized the critical moment. Her response could mean life or death for everyone remaining aboard. "Dennis. What do you want me to do, dear?"

"I want you to stay."

Mary reached out, rubbing his hand gently. "OK. I'll stay with you, Dennis." Her psychiatric training told her to maintain the connection, to keep him feeling understood and in control.

His next words sent a chill through her. "You understand if you come with me back up in the air we're going into oblivion."

"Yes. I know, dear." Mary's response was calm, though her heart raced at the implications.

"Thank you."

Mary saw an opportunity to make a strategic move. "May I go to the washroom, Dennis?"

"Sure"

She carefully handed the wires to Cini and headed toward the facilities. She briefly glanced back and just as Cini turned to John she ducked into the galley instead.

Cini pointed at the floor in front of him and ordered John. "Get down on your knees here."

John obliged and Cini pointed the shotgun at his head. Just then Phillip returned from the back of the plane.

"Did you see anyone?" Cini demanded.

"No one," replied Phillip. "I went through the plane on my hands and knees."

Mary returned to the lounge wearing a blonde wig – a subtle but significant change that she hoped would further cement her bond with Cini.

"See? I just had to freshen up. Do I look gorgeous?"

Cini's response was immediate and genuine. "I thought you looked gorgeous before."

Mary seized on his response, trying to maintain the lightness of the moment. "See John? Dennis says nice things to me. Why don't you?"

John's weak laugh was cut short as Cini raised the shotgun from where it had been pressed against his head. The hijacker's rapid mood swings were becoming more pronounced, his decisions more erratic.

"Go tell the captain to hurry up."

John headed to the cockpit. When Captain Ehman entered the lounge moments later, hands raised high above his head, his experienced eyes took in every detail of the scene – the money, the suitcase, Mary in her blonde wig, and the desperate man with the shotgun.

"Where do you want to go? Cuba?"

"No. I'll give you our destination once we're in the air."

"It will still take a little while longer to get a full fuel load," informed the captain.

"That's fine"

The captain's plea was simple but heartfelt. "We'll do everything you ask. Just don't harm the crew."

"Go back to the cockpit," Cini commanded.

Ehman turned, hands still in the air and headed back to the cockpit.

He sat back down in the left seat and put his headset on. "Air Canada 812 what's your destination?" ATC inquired.

"I don't know," the captain replied. "The guy says he'll tell me once we're in the air."

Ehman turned and looked at First Officer Hagenson and shrugs his shoulders. Just then John entered the cockpit.

"He wants to leave right now."

"Right now?" responded the captain. "But we're not finished fueling. We're only half full."

"He doesn't care," said John.

"Okay."

"Great Falls stop fueling. We're taking off without delay."

"Copy that 812," answered ATC.

The fuel trucks pulled away and the engines of the DC-8 roared to life. The aircraft did a 180, roared back down runway 03 and took off into the Montana night sky.

With John back in the lounge, Cini informed him of the destination.

"Go tell the captain we're going to New York."

John headed back to the cockpit and poked his head in.

He cleared his throat and said, "He says we're going to New York."

"Roger that," replied the captain.

As the DC-8 approached the service ceiling of 37,000 feet it starts a slow bank to head east towards The Big Apple. But before they'd even properly established their course, Cini changed his mind.

"Actually, tell the Captain to cancel New York. We're going to Phoenix, Arizona, and tell him I want to see him again," he told John.

Each shift in destination seemed to carry a deeper meaning, a hint of the internal struggle playing out behind his mask. They reflected Cini's deteriorating mental state, but Mary saw something else in his behavior – a man whose plan was unraveling, making him potentially more dangerous than ever. She caught John's eye briefly on his way back to the cockpit. A silent message passing between them: they needed to stay alert, to be ready for whatever came next. Mary suspected Cini's erratic commands were far from over. She continued holding the wires apart in her left hand, her fingers cramping but her resolve unchanged.

John enters the cockpit once again. "He wants you to head to Phoenix and he also wants to talk to you again."

Captain Ehman turned the controls over to First Officer Hagenson and got up out of his seat.

"Head to Phoenix Nels."

Chapter 13: The Escape Plan

Mary sensed an opportunity to deepen her connection with Cini. "It's alright now, Dennis. You're all alone now with your friends. Why don't you take your coat and wig off and just relax?"

"No. I promised them I wouldn't." The response was quick, almost defensive, suggesting to Mary that there were others involved in his plan – or perhaps just in his mind.

When Captain Ehman entered with his hands raised, Cini ordered John, Mary, and Phillip to move to economy class.

"OK, captain, put your hands down." The tension in his voice unmistakable. His demands shifted again. "I want to go back to Calgary, pick up a friend and finish fueling up." He paused, adding pointedly, "Leave the engines running."

Captain Ehman slowly lowered his arms. Maintaining his professional calm, he tried to reason with him about refueling times.

"Fine. But if we don't shut down all the engines to refuel it will take us about an hour. If we do, it will only take about 30 minutes."

Cini's eyes narrowed. "I'll let you know," he said curtly.

"And where to after Calgary?" Ehman pressed.

"I'll tell you after we take off," Cini stated flatly.

The captain drew himself up. "Listen," he began, "Wouldn't you like to perhaps discuss this with someone on the ground? This is a serious offense, you know. If you give yourself up now, the penalty will be less severe."

Cini remained silent, the twin barrels of the shotgun unwavering in their aim.

"I'll give you full use of the radio," Ehman offered, hoping to appeal to some sense of reason.

Cini's reaction was immediate and hostile. "I don't want to talk to anyone," he growled, the threat in his voice unmistakable.

"Okay then," Ehman conceded, realizing further persuasion was futile. "Back to Calgary it is." He turned and walked back to the cockpit.

In economy, John's whispered words to Mary carried both frustration and fear. "You're a fool. You should have got off when he gave you the chance."

"We're all going to die anyway," Mary replied, her tone suggesting she knew something John didn't.

"The hell we will." John's determination was fierce. He turned to Mary, outlining a desperate plan. "Listen, when he comes through the curtains, even if he shoots us, forget about the pain and just jump him. Keep an eye down the aisle through the curtains and if you see him coming, let us know."

Their planning was cut short as the hooded terrorist burst through the curtains.

"You," he said pointing the shotgun at Phillip. "Come with me."

Phillip got up.

"Head to the cockpit," Cini ordered. "I want to speak with the captain again."

Cini followed Phillip with the shotgun at his back to the cockpit. Phillip opened the door and headed in.

"Captain, Dennis would like to talk to you."

Phillip retreated and Cini walked in shotgun drawn. Ehman turned around, stood up from his seat and held his hands up.

"I want all your headsets," Cini ordered.

Ehman and the two other officers disconnected their equipment and handed them to him.

"Now," he said to the captain. "I want to talk to you again. Come with me."

Captain Ehman followed Cini back into the lounge.

The conversation that followed revealed Cini's true intentions. Pulling out an Air Canada DC-8 emergency card, Cini pointed to the interior diagram. "I want to bail out from the rear main door."

Ehman's response was measured, technical. "It's impossible. You can't open the door against the pressure."

"Fine. I'll blow the tail off then."

The captain's voice remained soft, reasonable, as he explained the fatal flaws in that plan. "It won't work. First of all, you might blow up with it. Second, the aircraft will go into a dive and you won't be able to scramble out the hole." He offered an alternative that might actually work. "The best thing to do is to go out an emergency window over a wing and then slide down off of it."

"I'll hit the tail."

"No you won't. The tail's well above the wing. Plus you'll drop coming off of it."

Cini paused squinting at Ehman skeptically.

"OK," he conceded. "But you'll have to decompress. I want you to drop to 3,000 feet above ground level and fly at 100 miles an hour."

The captain compromised. "We can take it to 3,000 feet but the minimum I can give you is 120 miles an hour or the plane will stall."

"Alright," Cini replied. "Do it."

Ehman returned to the cockpit and sat back down in his seat. He turned to Hagenson to share his realization.

"I think this nutbar has a parachute, Nels. He's asking to descend to 3,000 feet above ground and to pull her back to around 100 knots."

"Jesus," responded Hagenson.

Ehman pushed forward on the control column while pulling back on the throttle. As the massive DC-8 began its descent, the change in engine pitch marking their slow descent into the night sky, the crew knew they were entering the most dangerous phase of the hijacking. Cini's plan was becoming clear – he intended to parachute from the aircraft. With his explosives, shotgun, and increasingly unstable mental state, the next few minutes would determine whether anyone aboard Flight 812 would survive the night.

Suddenly Cini was standing behind them.

"Hurry up. I'll need some help opening the window," his impatience evident.

The captain started getting up out of his seat. "Take it down to 3,000 above ground and keep it steady," he instructed the FO. "Stay at 105 knots and be sure to keep the flaps full to cruise that slow."

"Yessir," replied Hagenson.

Ehman headed aft.

As Captain Ehman left his seat to help with the window, the tension in the aircraft was palpable. Everyone aboard knew that the next few minutes would either end in disaster or deliverance. The heavy blue suitcase's contents now made perfect sense – Cini had been planning this escape from the beginning.

Chapter 14: Breaking Point

Back in the dimly lit lounge, Cini was in his seat dancing his lighter flame dangerously close to the dynamite fuses. His blue suitcase lay open, revealing a parcel bound tightly with twine. The scene carried an air of deadly preparation.

"You have a knife?" Cini asked, his voice tense.

"No."

"I have to cut the twine on this parcel," urged Cini.

Captain Ehman measured his response carefully. "All we have is a safety axe in the cockpit."

"Get it," neither man fully realizing how that simple tool would soon change everything.

When Ehman returned with the axe, he handed it to Cini handle first, maintaining the appearance of cooperation while his mind raced through possible scenarios. "What's in there?" he asked, nodding toward the parcel.

"A parachute."

With the confirmation of Ehman's suspicions came new instructions. Cini handed the parcel to the captain.

"Take this and walk back to economy."

Cini walked behind him holding the headsets and axe in one hand, his shotgun in the other.

As they approached economy class, Phillip, back in his seat, spied them through the crack in the curtain. His whispered warning cut through the tension. "It's the captain. Don't do anything."

As they walked in, Cini waved his gun at the seated crew.

"You three get out," he ordered. "Go back to the front."

As Cini prodded Ehman toward the emergency window a few rows further into economy, John made his move, ducking down on the floor unnoticed.

Ehman set the parcel down on the seat beside the emergency window and Cini tossed the headsets on the seat beside that. He then tried to cut the twine with the axe with one hand while maintaining his grip on the shotgun with the other which was completely futile.

The instant he set the weapon down on the seat, the cabin erupted into chaos.

Ehman's move was lightning-fast. In one fluid motion he sent the shotgun flying down the aisle and pounded on Cini's forearm holding the axe which fell. He lunged for Cini's throat, both thumbs driving into the sky pirate's windpipe. Cini's eyes bulged with shock and rage.

"What the hell!?!" he choked out, his voice a gurgling rasp.

Despite Ehman's height advantage he had a hard time containing him as Cini fought back like a cornered animal. The captain's cry for help brought John swooping in, grabbing Cini's arms from behind. Suddenly he went limp.

"Get in here!" the captain hollered. "We need help!"

Phillip ran in.

"Get some duct tape," the captain instructed. "We gotta tie him up."

Phillip ran back out.

Just as they thought they had him subdued, he exploded into motion again seconds later. In an instant, Cini started thrashing madly. He managed to free an arm and thrust it into his pocket. His intention was clear. "I'll blow you bastards up!!!"

John grabbed his arm again and ripped the stick of dynamite out of his hand. Ehman had a firm grasp on his other arm.

As they stripped away his disguise – the wig, the hood, the poorly glued false mustache – Cini's true face emerged, contorted with rage and streaming with sweat. His eyes were wild circles of terror.

When Phillip returned with the duct tape, Cini started a new bout of screaming and violent resistance. The captain's order came sharp and desperate:

"Hit him Phillip! Hit him with the axe!"

The sound of the blunt end of the axe striking Cini's skull was sickening, but somehow after a couple of blows he managed to stay on his feet, blood streaming down his face. His superhuman determination became clear as even the sharp edge of the blade couldn't stop his frenzied resistance. Cini kept fighting, struggling with unnatural strength.

"Use the handle!" yelled the captain.

It was only when Phillip landed a crushing blow with a nauseating crunch, did Cini finally collapse onto the seat on top of the headsets.

Second Officer Belanger burst in with more tape from the cockpit.

"Better late than never Noel," exclaimed the captain completely out of breath. "Tape him up. And tape him good."

Ehman grabbed the headsets and headed back to the cockpit.

The next few minutes was a blur of motion and tape as the three crew members secured their unconscious prisoner to the seat. When they finished, Cini resembled a grey-wrapped mummy.

John's wink to Noel and Phillip carried exhaustion, relief, and disbelief. "Whew. Well, I think that oughta do it."

The victory felt surreal – their ordeal transformed in mere minutes from psychological warfare to brutal physical combat. As the adrenaline began to fade, the reality of what they'd just accomplished started to sink in. They had taken down a terrorist armed with dynamite and a shotgun, armed with nothing but desperation and a safety axe. Blood slowly dripped down the grey duct tape, a stark reminder of how close they'd all come to a very different ending.

Chapter 15: Aftermath

Captain Ehman's voice was tempered by both relief and exhaustion as he radioed ATC: "Calgary tower, this is Air Canada 812. We have subdued the hijacker. Requesting to land."

The response was urgent. "Roger Air Canada 812. You better hurry. There's heavy fog incoming. All other planes are being diverted." A pause, then: "You're cleared straight in on 35 left. Due to the explosives onboard, do not approach the terminal. Taxi left to runway 11 and hold."

The massive DC-8 touched down in the thick pea soup fog, taxied to runway 11 and stopped. Ehman shut all the engines down and looked at his watch – midnight on the nose. The fourteen-hour ordeal was finally over. He let out a heavy sigh, unbuckled his seatbelt and stood up.

"Let's get the hell out of here," he said emphatically. "Head office has a Chinese food spread and liquor waiting for us all at The Calgary Inn."

"You'll get no argument from me," Hagenson agreed.

As the crew prepared to depart, Mary stopped the incoming RCMP officers and explosives expert with a warning. "There's a package full of dynamite back there with the hijacker. He said the two wires sticking out will blow the plane up if they touch. Be careful lads."

The aftermath unfolded like scenes from a surreal movie: Cini, unconscious and bound, being carried off like a grey limp mummy to a waiting ambulance; the careful examination of the Woolco bag revealing 6 more sticks of dynamite and the final, ironic truth – the wires Mary had held apart terrorizing her for hours had never been connected to anything. Just two wires twisted together. Cini's threat of detonation had been nothing but an elaborate bluff. His blue suitcase, blown open with a stick of dynamite on the tarmac, told its own story of meticulous planning. Among the items recovered:

- A pair of goggles with extra lenses
- A sheepskin rope
- A five-band transistor radio
- A flashlight
- Hiking boots
- A water canteen
- A plastic bag filled with clothing
- Two Air Canada schedules
- A collapsible shovel
- A map of the world
- Photographs of parachute jumpers
- A bag of chocolate bars
- Paperback copies of "Airport" and "Hijacked"
- A .30-calibre US Army issued folding carbine
- ID cards in the name of Dennis A Munro

But Cini's story wasn't over. A week after being remanded to the Ponoka Mental Hospital in Alberta while he awaited trial, he escaped through a bathroom window in the middle of the night. Wearing only light blue scrubs and slippers in -20°C weather, he made it nearly an hour down the highway toward Red Deer which was nearly 60km away before being recaptured by the RCMP, shivering and begging to be taken back to the warmth of the hospital.

Epilogue: Legacy

The warm overcast morning of July 22nd, 2017 in Bay de Verde, a small fishing community on the northern tip of Newfoundland's Avalon Peninsula, carried the salt of the ocean and the weight of history. As the priest sprinkled holy water on Mary Dohey's black cloth covered urn, plumes of sea spray from a group of whales frolicking nearby rose into the air. Even they seemed to be paying tribute to a fallen hero.

"Born in St. Bride's Newfoundland on September 22nd, 1933, Mary Imelda Dohey was the youngest of 14 children," the priest intoned. He recounted her difficult childhood – losing her mother at three, the harsh years in foster care, the orphanage, and finally adoption at ten. "Mary went on to train as a psychiatric nurse," he continued, "which became an invaluable resource for her later career as a long-time flight attendant with Air Canada."

The priest's final words carried across the cemetery: "In November 1971 aboard Air Canada Flight 812, she used these skills she learned and thanks to her sheer grit and nerves of steel, Mary would go on to save over a hundred lives, thousands of feet in the air. For that we thank you, Mary. You are a true Canadian Hero. May you finally rest in peace."

The standing ovation that followed seemed to echo across the decades, a tribute to a woman whose courage and compassion had changed the course of aviation history.

In the years following the hijacking:

- Paul Joseph Cini was charged and sentenced to four life terms for hijacking, 14 years for extortion and 10 years for illegal possession of dynamite and a prohibited weapon. He was paroled just ten years later for good behaviour. He went on to change his name and settle down in Calgary with a wife and children.

- Less than two weeks after the hijacking an unidentified man who infamously became known as "D.B. Cooper" hijacked Northwest Orient Flight 305 armed with a bomb. After receiving $200,000 ransom money, he parachuted out of the tail of the Boeing 727 into the night over a remote wooded area of Washington State never to be seen again.
- Over the course of the next 8 months there were 12 copycat parachute hijackings in the US. Only 5 of which the hijacker made it to the ground successfully. The rest were apprehended by the FBI or flight crews before they could jump.
- All Irish detainees were eventually released from the British internment camps. This dark period of time in Ireland's history became known as "The Troubles".
- On December 1st 1975, stewardess Mary Dohey became the first living recipient of the Cross of Valour, Canada's highest honour for bravery. She was recognized by both Queen Elizabeth II and Prime Minister Pierre Trudeau. Mary continued her career as a flight attendant, finally retiring in 1991, even though she suffered from nightmares and fears which is now commonly known as PTSD.
- John Arpin received the Star of Courage, and Captain Vernon Ehman the Medal of Bravery. The second and third highest awards Canada can bestow for bravery respectively.
- The era of airliner hijackings ended as airport security transformed worldwide with the introduction of metal detectors, x-ray machines, and careful passenger screening.

But perhaps the most lasting legacy was the reminder that ordinary people, faced with extraordinary circumstances, can find within themselves the courage to save not only their own lives but the lives of others. Mary Dohey's childhood prayer in the orphanage – "Lord, please don't let me die in vain" – had been answered in ways she could never have imagined.

Under the white cross marking her final resting place, the simple epitaph seemed to capture it all: "A humble hero who found strength in compassion."

"This book is based on actual events. Some characters are fictional and some portions and dialogue are invented for creative and storyline purposes."

HAPPY PASSENGERS AFTER HIJACK ORDEAL
. . . aboard bus on way to hotels in Great Falls after second landing

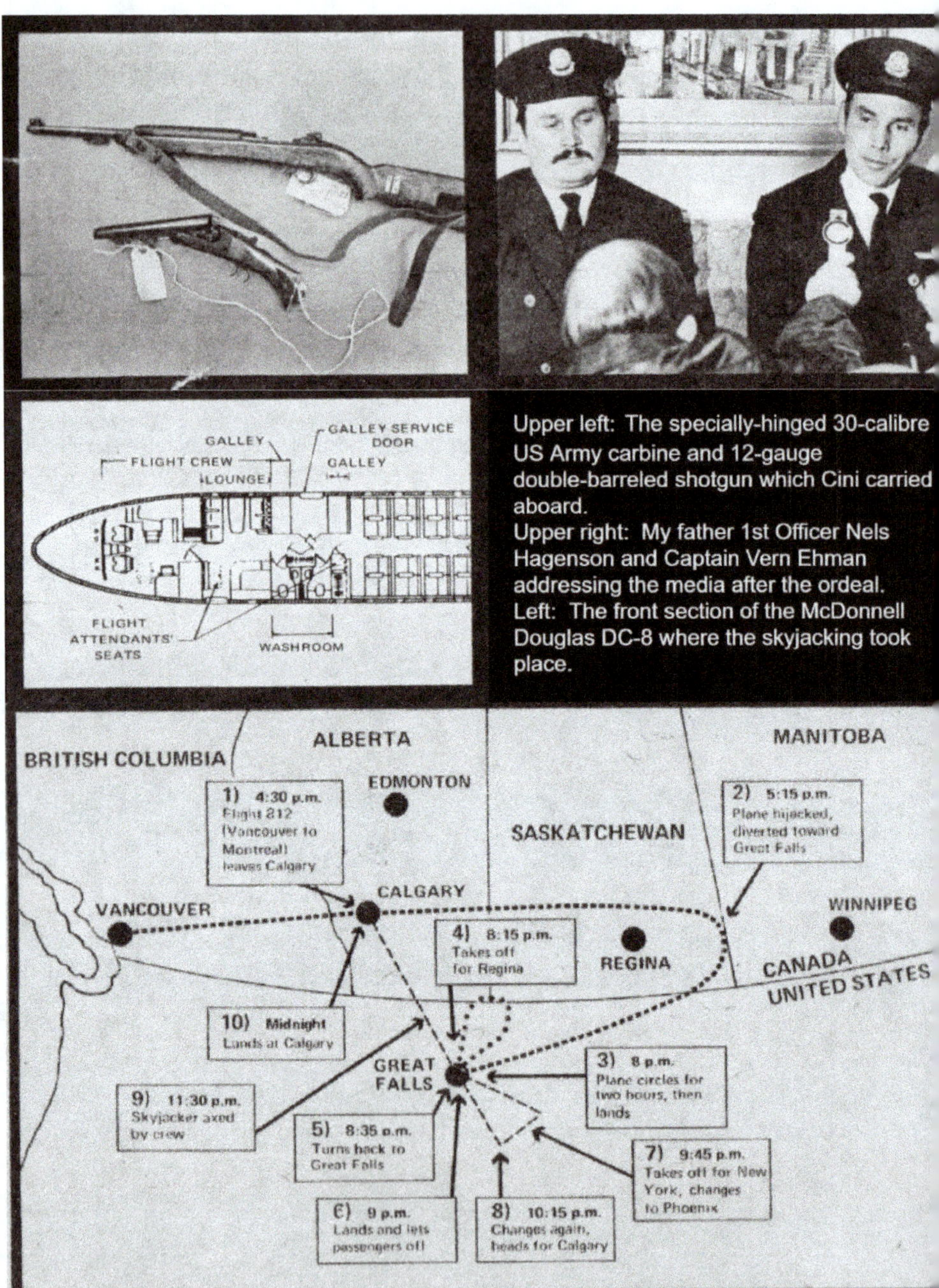

Upper left: The specially-hinged 30-calibre US Army carbine and 12-gauge double-barreled shotgun which Cini carried aboard.

Upper right: My father 1st Officer Nels Hagenson and Captain Vern Ehman addressing the media after the ordeal.

Left: The front section of the McDonnell Douglas DC-8 where the skyjacking took place.

WEEKEND MAGAZINE

The Sunday Sun

1871 1971

CREW TELLS OF HIJACKING:

'I'll blow you all up'

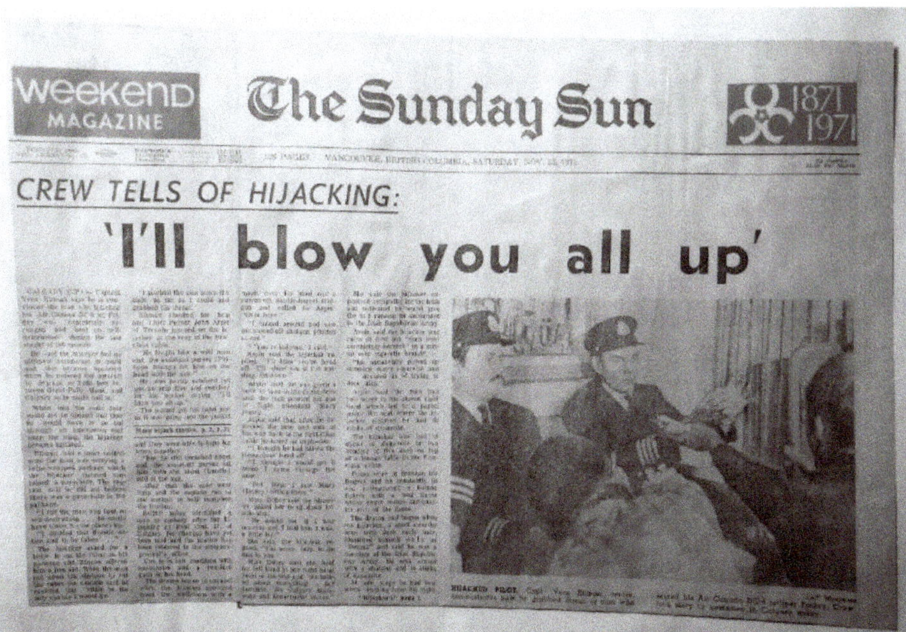

Dad on the left and Captain Ehman debriefing the media after the hijacking on the cover of the Vancouver Sun

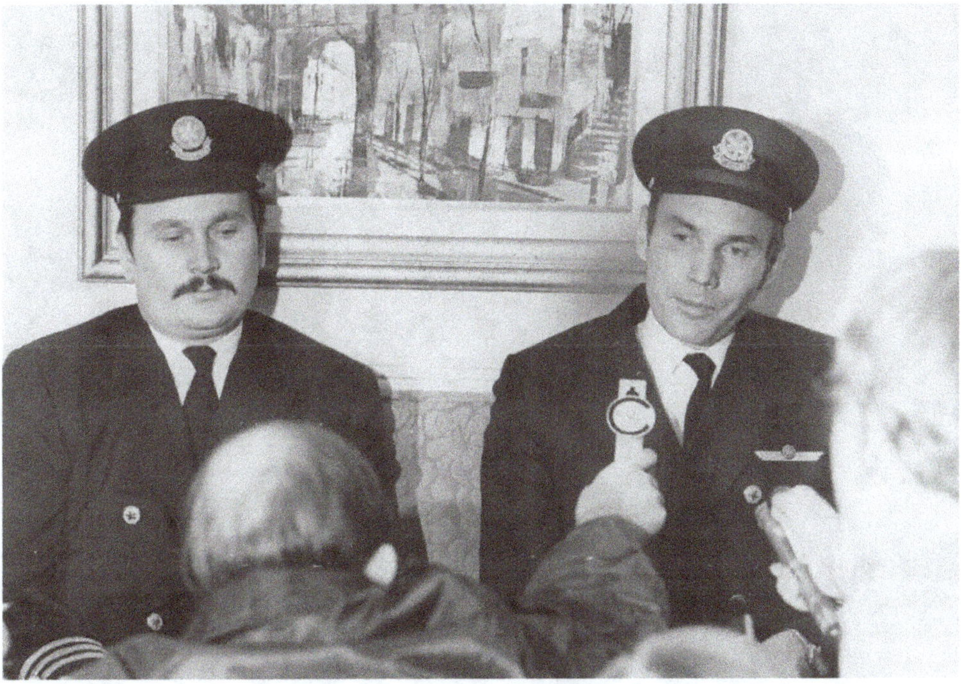

Mary Dohey after the ordeal. Still unnerved after hours of having a shotgun at her temple and holding wires apart that she thought were tethered to live explosives. Purser John Arpin at her side who was ordered to hold dynamite in his mouth.

Mary receiving the Cross of Valour from Canadian Prime Minister
Pierre Elliott Trudeau and
Queen Elizabeth II on December 1st, 1975.

Mary sporting her medal for Trudeau and the Queen

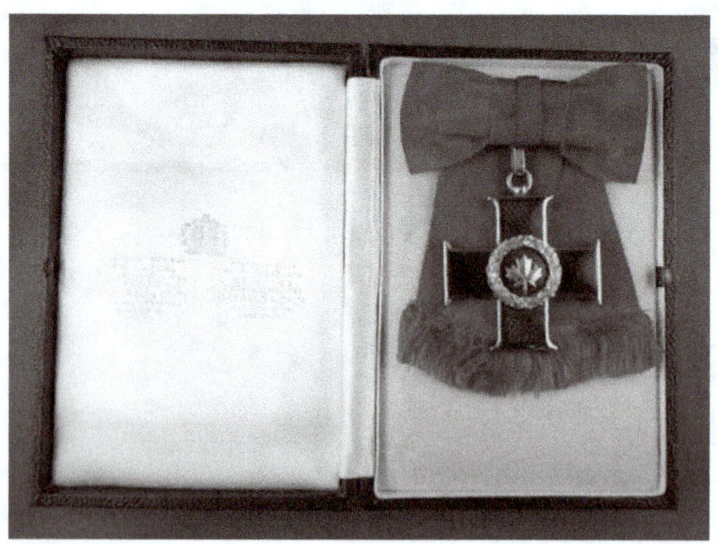

Mary and her guest, Sister Mary Electa with Governor General Jules Leger and Gabrielle Leger shortly after receiving the Cross of Valour

A truly beautiful medal for an amazing lady. Mary's a real Canadian hero.

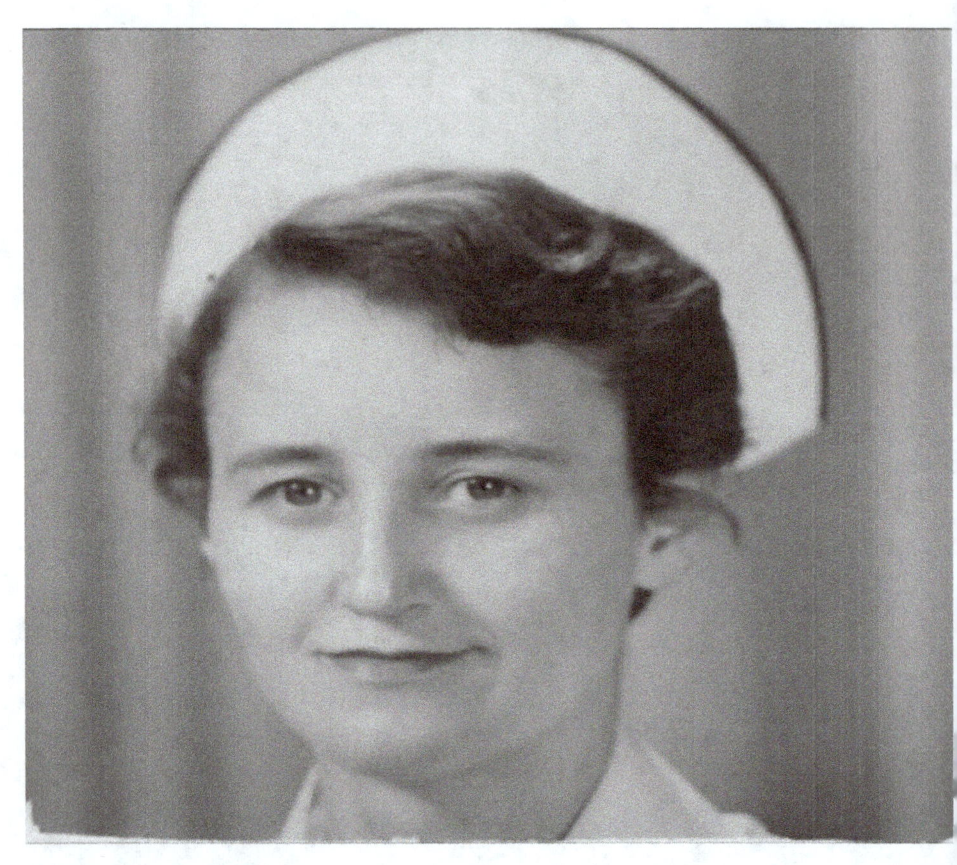

Mary during her nursing training

**Mary as a young Trans-Canada Air Lines stewardess
before it became Air Canada in 1965**

An Air Canada McDonnell Douglas DC-8 in the exact same livery as Flight 812. It may very well be the same plane but it's hard to make out the tail number.

**The Ponoka Mental Hospital from which Cini
temporarily escaped.**

Afterword

In the 1980's I discovered a large scrapbook tucked away in our
basement that my Grandmother Ada Hagenson had curated in the 70's
about her son Nels' hijacking. It was stuffed full of newspaper
headlines and clippings from across the country and just about
anything else she got her hands on pertaining to the event. Even things
like the menu from the gala that Air Canada threw for the crew
celebrating their heroism. I poured over it for hours and then put it
back in its spot amongst the rest of the forgotten albums and photos of
times gone by. So there it sat for a couple of decades until in 2022
when I rediscovered it again.

*A painting of an AC McDonnell Douglas DC-8 from the era on the
cover*

So here's a bit of an epilogue using some of those bits and pieces she collected. I'll explain them as we go. Enjoy.

Firstly, check this out. There were actually 3 Montreal detectives on board. They didn't know about the hijacking for hours. I think it was John Arpin who must've told them to just chill…

6 EDMONTON JOURNAL, Monday, November 15, 1971

3 detectives weren't told hijacking was in progress

MONTREAL (CP) — Three Montreal detectives, passengers aboard the hijacked Air Canada flight from Calgary Friday night, said they were not told for two hours that an armed man had commandeered the plane.

Capt. Ellis Leblanc said he and Sgt. Gilles Turcott and Sgt. Raymond Rajotte had been on a "regular investigation" out west. They returned home on a relief flight today with 18 other passengers.

Capt. Leblanc said he and his two men were enjoying an after-dinner drink in the economy section of the plane when they heard a brief explosion up front near the cockpit.

"We didn't know what it was at first but it sounded like a shot," he said in a telephone interview with the Montreal Star from Great Falls, Mont., prior to returning here.

Minutes later the steward came down the aisle collecting the glasses and told the passengers "a little something is wrong but we can't tell you what it is right now."

Capt. Leblanc said he considered what he and his men could do "whatever the situation," but before they could do anything they were approached by the steward who had noticed from the passenger list that they were policemen.

"He told us not to move or try anything because it may not have been safe for us and the other passengers. But at that time we still didn't know what was happening. The steward wouldn't tell us."

About 90 minutes later a stewardess announced to passengers in each section that a hijacking was in progress and that the plane was en route to Montana.

"Everyone took it in stride," said Capt. Leblanc. "There was no panic except for a woman near us with a small child. But she calmed down after a while."

Capt. Leblanc said after the 118 passengers disembarked at Great Falls, Mont., that the hijacking wasn't very exciting.

"I thought we would be going to Cuba or somewhere like that."

Another interesting fact is that Cini supposedly had absolutely no contact or affiliation with the IRA (or did he?) according to Sean Kenny, the joint general secretary for the IRA's political wing Sinn Fein. Curiously Mr. Kenny was in Vancouver on a fundraising and speaking tour at the time of the hijacking. Check it out…

IRA spokesman unable to talk to hijacker

The North American spokesman for the Irish Republican Army agreed Friday to try to talk the hijacker of an Air Canada DC-8 out of his plan to fly to Ireland.

But the airline turned down the idea, saying the hijacker was "unreachable."

In Vancouver on a fund-raising and speaking tour, Sean Kenny, joint general secretary for the IRA's political wing, Sinn Fein, said the organization would never condone hijackings or accept money obtained from such acts.

Before his speech at John Oliver High School a Sun reporter asked Kenny if he would talk to the hijacker if it could be arranged.

He conferred with four members of the Friends of Irish Freedom, a local group which organized his Vancouver visit, and said he would help if needed.

While Kenny addressed 400 people at the school, his offer was relayed to Air Canada by The Sun.

Airline officials discussed the idea with department of transport officials at Vancouver airport while the DC-8 circled over Great Falls, Mont. The offer was rejected.

"The situation is much too tense to try something like that," the airline spokesman said.

Following his address

Kenny denied that his speaking tour may have led the hijacker to act.

"If he had read the news reports or heard anything I said, he would have known hijacking could not be supported."

He predicted the British will play up the hijacker's reference to Ireland but said it would not have any long-term detrimental effects on the organization.

The Vancouver visit netted the IRA about $500 and the Canadian tour will bring an estimated $7,000 to $10,000, Kenny said.

IRA head disclaims hijacker

VANCOUVER (CP) — Sean Kenny, North American leader of the Irish Republican Army, said Friday night there was no connection between the IRA and the hijacking of an Air Canada DC-8 jetliner to Great Falls, Mont.

The man who hijacked the Vancouver-to-Toronto jetliner in Western Canada late Friday claimed to be a member of the IRA.

Mr. Kenny, joint general secretary of Sinn Fein, the political arm of the IRA, said "this hijacking has no connection w i t h the IRA whatsoever."

"It's tragic, it's a bad act," said Mr. Kenny, in Vancouver on a North American tour to raise funds for the IRA.

"We don't go along with hijacking or hijackers," he said. "Our job is to organize the working class people of Northern Ireland in their struggle. Terrorizing innocent people aboard airplanes has no part of that mission."

He said the hijacker must be "some nut or something."

"Anyone who wants to fly to Ireland with all its troubles has got to be sick."

Here's Dad's official report to Air Canada:

Inter-Office Correspondence

Place/Date	Vancouver, November 1971
Our File	
Your File	
Subject	Hijacking Incident, Flight 812-12 November

Flight Operations Director - Vancouver

I was operating Flight 812-12 November scheduled YVR/YYC/YYZ/YUL.
Flight departed Vancouver on routine schedule at 2130 GMT. Flight to
Calgary was routine. Off Calgary at 2325 GMT. At 12000 feet climbing
the Second Officer J.N. Belanger changed seats with me to climb to
cruising level of 37000 feet.

East of Lumsden, enroute Langruth the senior Purser J.J. Arpin came
forward with a note and stated, "We are being hijacked". He stated,
"the man has a gun and dynamite and we are to follow instructions".
The instructions were printed on two sides of 8½ x 11 writing paper.

The instructions advised us to proceed to Great Falls, Montana, obtain
1.5 million dollars ransom, then proceed to Regina where the passengers
would be allowed to disembark, and baggage deplaned so that a full load
of fuel could be boarded for a flight to Ireland. The note contained
threats that the hijacker was an IRA member, willing to die for his
cause. In fact, he stated he knew he would be killed in Ireland but
didn't care so it was up to us if we wanted to live. Also mentioned
was the Boston incident where the F/O was killed and not to try any
similar heroics.

I changed seats with the S/O and we resumed our normal positions and
duties. Clearance was obtained to proceed to Great Falls and Company
was advised via Regina company radio. Either just prior to this
reversal of course or shortly after, there was the sound of an explosion. We put on our oxygen masks and selected "emerg" anticipating
rapid depressurization. The Purser came forward and advised that the
hijacker had fired his sawed off shotgun into the panel between the
first class lounge and flight deck. Pellets reached pilot area.

Enroute to Great Falls we advised Air Canada of these developments,
particularly the urgency of the ransom money. In range of Great Falls
communication was established with company on an ARINC patch. Overhead
Great Falls we estimated one hour 40 mins. holding fuel with a safe
reserve for letdown and landing. We commenced a very wide hold on the
288° radial of Great Falls with shallow turns so as not to alert the
hijacker that we were holding.

ACF424(2-65)

During this time we were arranging a location for refueling and for
the money transfer. (To be delivered in a suitcase, by a woman, and
to be hoisted up by a rope through the forward cabin door.)

The door was to be opened only partially to allow the suitcase through,
so that she would not be able to identify him. Also, the hijacker
would allow us a maximum of 15 minutes ground time, and we were not
to shut down the engines. However we shut down one and two engines
to allow the lady and refuelers to approach in safety.

As soon as the money was counted by the Purser the hijacker became
extremely nervous and insisted that we take off. The Purser advised
us that there was not 1.5 million dollars in the suitcase, but by the
clever adjustment of figures he had arrived at a 1.5 million total. We
had landed at 0315 GMT, shutdown at 0320, disconnected tender and
commenced start of engines one and two at 0332, airborne at 34 enroute
to Regina, "we thought"

At 150 n. miles DME from Great Falls the hijacker advised us via
message from the Purser to return to Great Falls. He wanted to see
an airport sign indicating Great Falls which he had not seen on our
first landing. He promised to let the passengers and luggage off.
Clearance obtained we returned. Great Falls was advised to provide
the stand to evacuate the aircraft and refueling presumably for a
destination of Ireland.

With the passengers off our hijacker wanted us airborne. He seemed
uncertain of destination or at least unwilling to tell us on the
ground. The Captain, V.L. Ehman asked if he could go aft to speak to
the hijacker. Prior to this he had refused to allow any pilot aft
and had only allowed a Purser forward for a moment to pass a message.

Captain Ehman returned to the cockpit and advised that he thought the
man was desperate but also very nervous and that it would be best to
comply and get airborne immediately. Times on, in, out and off were
0438, 0443, 0525, 0530 GMT. We had shut down number 3 and 4 engines
for this operation.

When airborne we were advised to proceed to Phoenix. During climb the
hijacker again allowed the Captain back to talk to him. At this time
he had placed the Purser, Assistant Purser P.R. Bonny and Senior
Stewardess M.I. Dohey in the front row of the economy cabin and closed
the curtain. I believe the Captain was able to persuade the hijacker
to change his mind and return to Calgary.

Place/Date
Our File
Your File
Subject Hijacking Incident, Flight 812-12 November, continued 3.

When the Captain returned to the cockpit, this time accompanied by hijacker, he advised us that the hijacker had now changed his mind and was going to jump at some distance from Calgary.

The hijacker made us give him all the headsets and mi ophones from the cockpit so that no air-ground communication would be possible. Descent was commenced early approaching Calgary. Approximately 40 miles south of Calgary the aircraft was depressurized at 3000 feet above ground. Airspeed was reduced to 100 knots as requested by the hijacker for his parachute jump.

The hijacket requested that one cockpit crew member proceed aft to assist him. Also he wanted a knife to cut the strong cord on the package that supposedly contained his parachute. The Captain suggested the use of the fire axe for this. The hijacker proceeded aft, carrying the fire axe and sawed-off shotgun, with Captain Ehman carrying the parcel. Before leaving the cockpit the Captain whispered "I might try anything". The Second Officer occupied the Captain's seat at this time. Shortly the Assistant Purser yelled "We've got him". I told the Second Officer, "Take the tape and go back and help".

We now turned up the speakers to obtain landing information. The Captain returned to his seat and the S/O brought up a microphone which was plugged in at the auxiliary panel, the forward position being damaged when it was disconnected. The S/O advised Calgary that we had control of the aircraft and obtained landing clearance. We landed on R/16 and dispersed to a point designated on R/07, north of the terminal building. At this point the a/c was shut down and ground personnel and RCMP took over.

N.G. Hagenson
First Officer

ACF424(2-65)

Air Canada put on a big spread for the crew about 10 days later at the lavish Queen Elizabeth Hotel in Montreal. The city where Air Canada headquarters is located. Here's the crew. Dad on the far left, Captain Ehman in the middle with Mary Dohey on his left, John Arpin on the far right…

Dad having a good time with his date Vivian Lemonde.

Dad and Vivian on the left. Stewardess Pamela Windebank in the middle who was also onboard.

The menu…

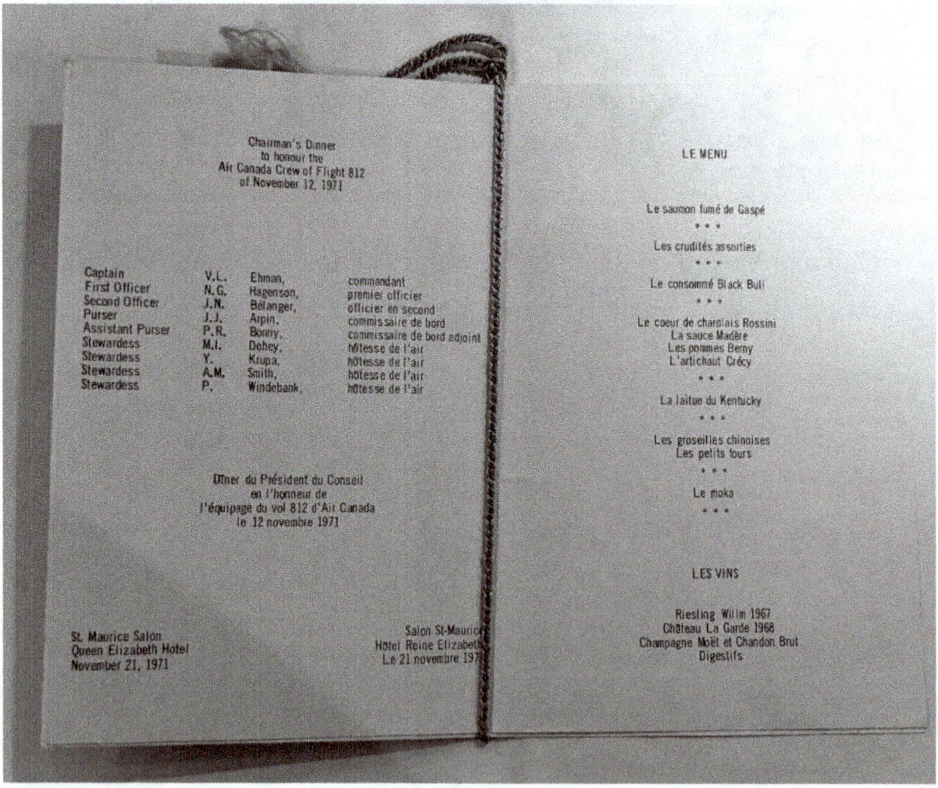

Chairman's Dinner
to honour the
Air Canada Crew of Flight 812
of November 12, 1971

Captain	V.L.	Ehman,	commandant
First Officer	N.G.	Hagenson,	premier officier
Second Officer	J.N.	Bélanger,	officier en second
Purser	J.J.	Arpin,	commissaire de bord
Assistant Purser	P.R.	Bonny,	commissaire de bord adjoint
Stewardess	M.I.	Dohey,	hôtesse de l'air
Stewardess	Y.	Krupa,	hôtesse de l'air
Stewardess	A.M.	Smith,	hôtesse de l'air
Stewardess	P.	Windebank,	hôtesse de l'air

Dîner du Président du Conseil
en l'honneur de
l'équipage du vol 812 d'Air Canada
le 12 novembre 1971

St. Maurice Salon
Queen Elizabeth Hotel
November 21, 1971

Salon St-Maurice
Hôtel Reine Elizabeth
Le 21 novembre 1971

LE MENU

Le saumon fumé de Gaspé
* * *
Les crudités assorties
* * *
Le consommé Black Bull
* * *
Le cœur de charolais Rossini
La sauce Madère
Les pommes Berny
L'artichaut Crécy
* * *
La laitue du Kentucky
* * *
Les groseilles chinoises
Les petits fours
* * *
Le moka
* * *

LES VINS

Riesling Willm 1967
Château La Garde 1968
Champagne Moët et Chandon Brut
Digestifs

A couple of letters of commendation came in from the higher ups at the company…

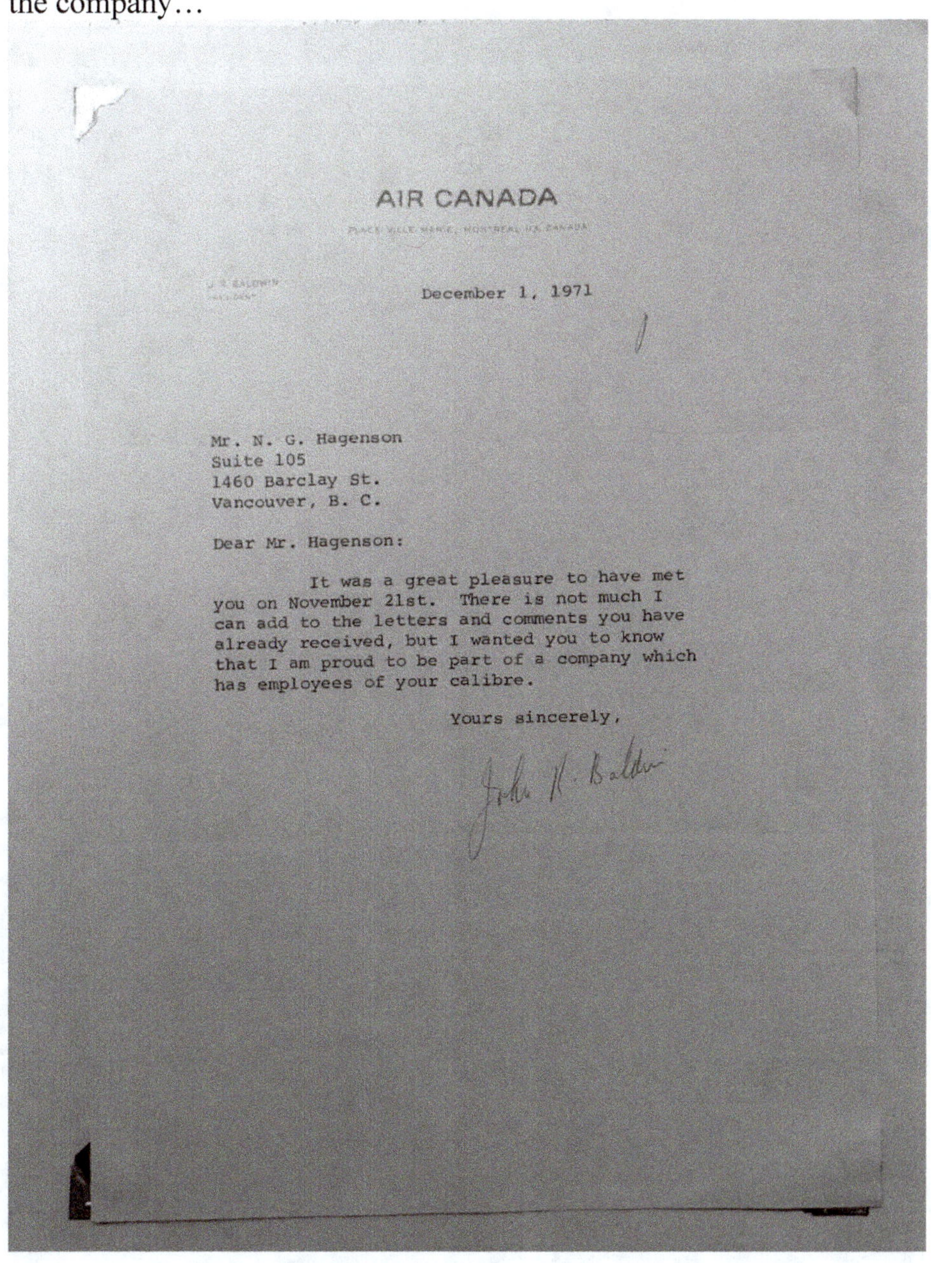

AIR CANADA
PLACE VILLE MARIE, MONTREAL 113, CANADA

J. R. BALDWIN
PRESIDENT

December 1, 1971

Mr. N. G. Hagenson
Suite 105
1460 Barclay St.
Vancouver, B. C.

Dear Mr. Hagenson:

    It was a great pleasure to have met you on November 21st. There is not much I can add to the letters and comments you have already received, but I wanted you to know that I am proud to be part of a company which has employees of your calibre.

    Yours sincerely,

John R. Baldwin

AIR CANADA

PLACE VILLE-MARIE, MONTREAL 113, CANADA

YVES PRATTE
PRÉSIDENT DU CONSEIL ET DIRECTEUR GÉNÉRAL
CHAIRMAN AND CHIEF EXECUTIVE OFFICER

November 30, 1971

Mr. N.G. Hagenson,
Suite 105,
1460 Barclay St.
Vancouver, B.C.

Dear Mr. Hagenson,

I wish to say how pleased my wife and I were to meet you and Miss Vivian Lemonde at our little get-together Sunday the 21st.

I thought you might like to receive the enclosed photographs as another souvenir of what was for us a most pleasant evening.

My best regards to you and Miss Lemonde.

Yours sincerely,

Soon after passenger letters of appreciation starting pouring in for the crew. Here's a few…

Montreal International Airport, Dorval – December 15, 1971
PF/VLE; PF/JAB; 1741-1

Commendations from Passengers – Flt. 812/12 November

Captain V.L. Ehman

Air Canada – Montreal Base

Second Officer J.A. Belanger

Air Canada – Montreal Base

– – – – – – – – – – – – – – – – –

We are attaching copies of letters from passengers concerning

the above mentioned flight for your information.

May we again add our deep appreciation in this matter.

N.J. Logan
Flight Operations Director

cc: Flight Operations Director, Air Canada – Vancouver Base

/jh

November 19, 1971

Mr. Yves Pratte
Chairman & Chief Executive
Air Canada
Siege Social
Place Ville Marie
Montreal 113
Quebec

Dear Mr. Pratte:

In my capacity as Executive Vice-President & Marketing Manager of this Company,
I have, during the past several years, been a frequent user of airline facilities
in North America, The Far East, Europe and The British Isles; and during the
course of my travels I have experienced many pleasant and memorable happenings,
and also, while by far in the minority some not so pleasant ones.

However, the most memorable one has to be my personal experience on your Flight
No. 812 from Calgary to Toronto on Friday November 12th 1971 (via Great Falls,
Montana) which flight will long be remembered by me.

Having been personally involved, I naturally have read the news accounts and
watched the T.V. reports on this happening with more than considerable interest;
and while the event was given detailed exposure by all of the Media, I must, in all
conscience state that in my personal opinion, the Aircraft Crew and in particular
the Cabin Crew, who were the heroes of the piece, were not afforded the full credit
which is unquestionably due to them; and I sincerely trust that Air Canada will
make up for this deficiency by affording them in a tangible way, the full recognition
and appreciation which is their due.

The cool and very concise manner in which these people dealt with the literally
most explosive situation, and their collective handling of the in-flight tension-
filled moments which unquestionably prevented mass hysteria and confusion that could
have precipitated a tragedy, is certainly worthy of the highest possible commendation;
and the climatic orderly and uneventful unloading of the aircraft row by row after
the second landing, is indeed almost unbelievable under the particular circumstances
and is a tribute to these wonderful crew members and very definite credit to
Air Canada.

I am certain that there are many who share my opinion and while I will not presume
to speak on their behalf, I would respectfully request that you accept, on my
behalf for conveyance to the crew concerned, my most sincere personal thanks
and deep appreciation for their courageous conduct which possibly saved our lives.

(continued)

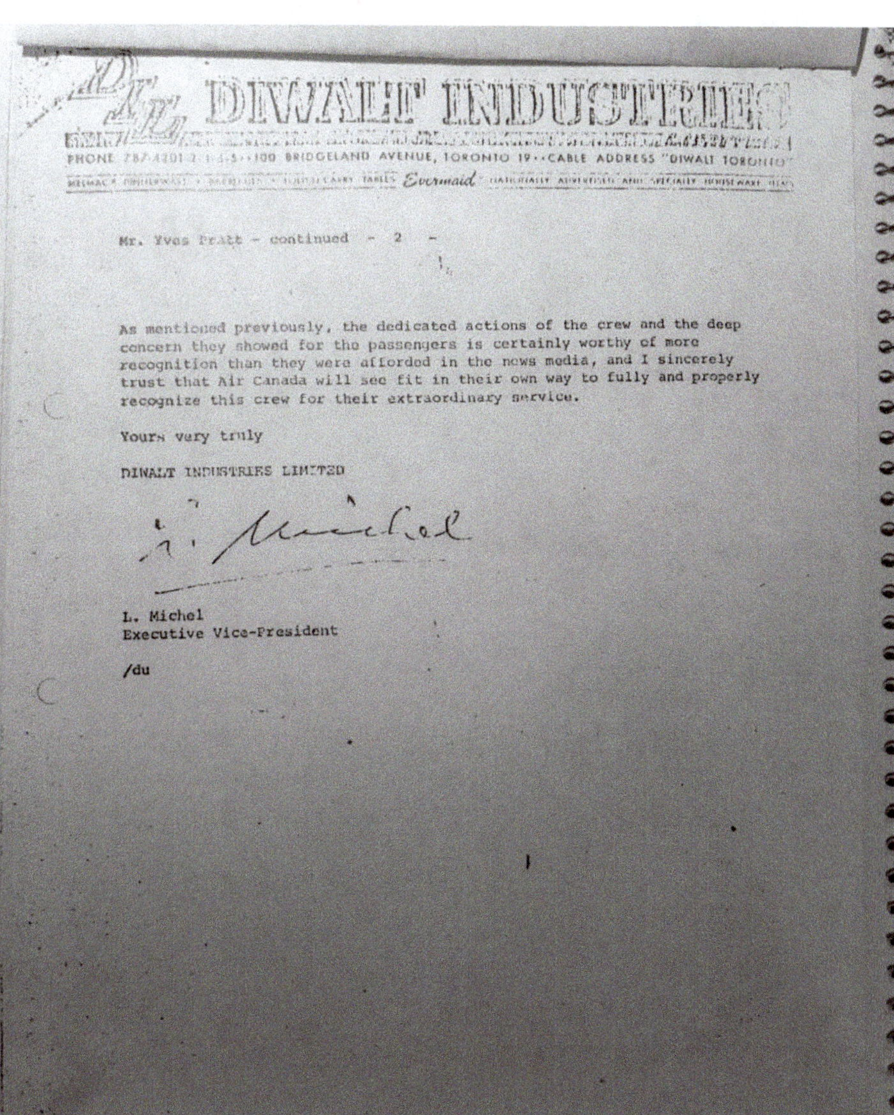

Mr. Yves Pratt — continued - 2 -

As mentioned previously, the dedicated actions of the crew and the deep
concern they showed for the passengers is certainly worthy of more
recognition than they were afforded in the news media, and I sincerely
trust that Air Canada will see fit in their own way to fully and properly
recognize this crew for their extraordinary service.

Yours very truly

DIWALT INDUSTRIES LIMITED

L. Michel
Executive Vice-President

/du

10 Parkway Forest Drive
Apartment #201
Willowdale, Ontario
November 26, 1971

Mr. J. R. Baldwin
President
Air Canada
Place Ville Marie
Montreal 113, Canada

Dear Sir:

Thank you for your letter of November 19, 1971.

I would like to express my appreciation for the way that Air
Canada's pilots, cabincrew and other personnel handled the
situation during the critical hours.

My assessment of my fellow passengers is the same as that
expressed by your air crew, however, the same must also
be said for the air crew and other Air Canada personnel,
who also were calm and level headed.

Your supervisor who met my wife and boy at Toronto Airport
and explained the situation to them deserves a lot of
credit too.

I might also add that the decision to send an aircraft
immediately to Great Falls to take us to Toronto was welcome
news and was much appreciated in my home.

Yours very truly,

J. Morch

JM/dg

P.S. - I am back in Calgary, but will
       be on Flight #812 to Toronto on
       December 23.

No reply
ANG

DEC - 6 1971

FRANZ PATELLA CONTRACTING LTD.

* CALGARY 24, ALBERTA – 1323 - 43RD AVENUE S.E. (403) 243-6040
EDMONTON, ALBERTA – 13025 - 149TH STREET, P.O. BOX 578, MAIN POST OFFICE (403) 455-4998
VANCOUVER, B.C. – P.O. BOX 2203 (604) 876-2822

OFFICES • PARTITIONS • ALTERATIONS • FINE WOODWORK

~~Dir~~ P.R
Dir Psgr Sales & Svcs.

December 2, 1971

Air Canada
Place Ville Marie
Montreal 113, Canada

Attention: Mr. J.R. Baldwin
President

Dear Mr. Baldwin:

I acknowledge with thanks receipt of your letter dated November 19, 1971 and wish to make the following comments concerning the hijacking of Flight 812 on November 12, 1971. I must say that a lot of credit goes to the crew and stewardesses for their excellent behavior in time of stress. Having gone through the Second World War, I was able to absorb the tremendous shock of such an incident and I feel that the other passengers reacted admirably. I am happy that everything ended up well and that no one got hurt.

My only wish is that there would be a change in law and any hijacker would definitely receive the death penalty for endangering the lives of hundreds of persons.

Yours very truly,

Franz Patella

Franz Patella

:jo

2624 Capital Hill ___ N.W.
Calgary, 44, Alta.,
Nov. 27, 1971

Mr. J. R. Baldwin, President,
Air Canada,
Montreal, Que.

Dear Sir,

After arriving in Toronto the children and I continued on with our planned trip in Toronto and area and arrived back home in Calgary a few days ago.

We were most thankful and grateful to the crew of Air Canada, Flight 812, Fri., Nov. 12th Calgary-Toronto for the manner in which they conducted themselves under very strained conditions. We deeply appreciate the concern shown for us, as well as your very kind letter.

Sincerely,

Mrs. K. E. Greenway

STANDARD SECURITIES LIMITED

655 Dixon Road, Skyline Hotel, Rexdale, Ontario. 416/248-6631

November 29, 1971.

Mr. J. R. Baldwin, President,
Air Canada,
Place Ville Marie,
Montreal, 113, Quebec.

Dear Mr. Baldwin:

Thank you for your letter of November 19th. I am sorry
that I have neglected writing until now. However, I would
like to say how much I appreciated the manner in which the
crew, stewards, and stewardesses conducted themselves during
the whole incident. They must be commended very highly,
particularly those who had to deal directly with the highjacker.

Sincerely,

J. Harry Frogley,

/jm

President
E. E. Lewis

Executive
Vice Presidents
J. Gardon
J. G. Lewis
G. R. Winthrope

Vice Presidents
M. Kessler
H. W. Norrington
G. C. Simpson

Sec.-Treasurer
S. J. C. Ellis

Directors
S. Assmith
B. Carmichael
T. H. Carmichael
H. Cole
F. Crossett
S. Eckler
M. Fox
J. H. Frogley
R. C. C. Henson
H. M. Hurst
J. Kinross
A. Tenney

Members/Toronto Stock Exchange/Canadian Stock Exchange

Twenty-one Shawfield Crescent
Don Mills 400, Ontario
Telephone (416) 444-9645

November 24, 1971.

Mr. J. R. Baldwin,
President,
Air Canada,
Place Ville Marie,
Montreal 113.

Dear Mr. Baldwin:

Thank you for your letter of November 19 concerning the
events which took place on Flight 812 on Friday, November 12.

I wish to express my thanks and gratitude to the entire
crew who behaved with great courage and resolution.
The captain and his flight crew who never lost their nerve
under very extreme stress deserve a very special praise.
I would like to commend, however, the Senior Purser
Mr. John Arpent who did his utmost to appease the hijacker
and at the same time maintain contact with the first class
passengers and administer to their needs and comforts.
My special thanks are due to him and I would appreciate it
if you could relay my sentiments to him.

Yours sincerely,

S. A. Rybb, P. Eng.

SAR:jj

So anyways, I thought to myself "I should do Grandma's efforts proud." Why don't we ever hear about this crazy piece of Canadiana? I have always really enjoyed a true story TV show on the Discovery Channel here in Canada called "Mayday: Air Disaster Investigation" which is kind of like the "Law & Order" of aviation (it's also aired in England with different narrators; etc.). It's an hour long show where the first half chronicles the disaster or crash and the second half the investigation and conclusion as to the cause of the disaster. I thought to myself that whoever creates this show would be perfect for retelling Dad's hijacking on the small or even big screen given all same types of interior and exterior aircraft shots that would be required. So after trying in vain to get in touch with any higher ups at the show I finally got a response from one of the predominant directors of the show. He had directed dozens of Maydays and really liked the story but needed to see some kind of treatment like a screenplay. So in October 2022 I took it upon myself to create a screenplay using all the source material that Grandma had so meticulously saved as well as whatever I could find online (there wasn't much). I mean, how hard could it be? I'm a big film buff and thought it would be a cool challenge. I did some research about formatting and I ended up utilizing a great piece of screenwriting software called Arc Studio. After picking away at it for nearly a year and a half it was finished. I forwarded it to the Mayday director who read it and he helped me with a few loose ends. Unfortunately by this time, in terms of getting it produced, he had a bunch of other projects on his plate and wasn't in a position to take it on. The summer of 2024 saw a real downturn in terms of new movie and TV show productions. It felt like it was going to be a hard sell. So I turned it into this "novella" which I hope you enjoyed. Hopefully someday the movie will come to fruition.

Sadly my Dad, retired Air Canada Captain Nels George Hagenson, FO in this story, passed away in July 2024 at the age of 83. Thankfully he was able to read my screenplay before he did and gave it his stamp of approval. Here's a bit about his illustrious aviation career.

Dad and a Harvard circa 1960

He grew up in eastern Alberta. After graduating from Edgerton High School in June 1959 Dad took a job as a truck driver at the Camp Wainwright army base for the summer. Then, in November 1959 at the tender age of 18, he enlisted as a trainee with the Royal Canadian Air Force (RCAF) at the air force base in Centralia, Ontario.

After a couple of months of ground school his first taste of flight was in a de Havilland Chipmunk on February 18 1960. Then, after just 13 flights with an instructor, he performed his first solo flight for 15 minutes on March 11. On March 25 he achieved his RCAF Primary Flying Certificate. He then moved to the Moose Jaw Air Force base for training in the Harvard aircraft. He was there from April until October 1960 when he received his Basic Flying Certificate. After Moose Jaw he went 2 hours north to RCAF Station Saskatoon where he flew the dual engine Beechcraft Expeditor from November 1960 to July 1966.

A Chipmunk Dad cut his flying teeth on

Dad with a Beechcraft Expeditor

After taking the summer off, he headed to Montreal to join the 438 Squadron in October 1966 ("The Wild Cats"). He flew the de Havilland Otter on wheels, floats and skis there pretty much exclusively. He even flew paratrooper drops. He was with the squadron until May 1969 at which point he received his Canadian Airline Transport Pilot license and started his career with Air Canada.

Dad started flying for Air Canada in August 1969 on the Vickers Viscount, a 4-engine turboprop airliner. He quickly moved to the McDonnell Douglas DC-8 jetliner which was what the hijacking took place on. From there he flew another 5 jet airliners during his career. The Boeing 727, Lockheed L1011-500 (his favourite), Boeing 767, Boeing 747 and retired on the Airbus A340. He flew for Air Canada for almost 35 years and was also the president of CALPA (the Canadian Airline Pilots Association) for a number of years.

His last flight was to Shanghai in 2001 accompanied by friends and family on the Airbus A340.

This was a plaque presented to Nels by his peers when he retired in 2001. It represented the 7 aircraft he flew during his career with Air Canada. The Vickars Viscount, McDonnell Douglas DC-8, Boeing 727, Lockheed L1011-500 (his favourite), Boeing 767, Boeing 747 and retiring on the Airbus A340. Can you identify them?

As you probably can tell by now, I created this book as not only a way for people to remember this forgotten piece Canadiana but to also honour my father's decades of service to Canada's aviation industry and history.

Ironically, in 2015, he decided it would be a good idea to skydive out of a perfectly good airplane for his 75th birthday. Here he is 10,000 feet over his retirement island of Tortola, British Virgin Islands in the Caribbean with his good buddy Lou. The guy sure had balls.

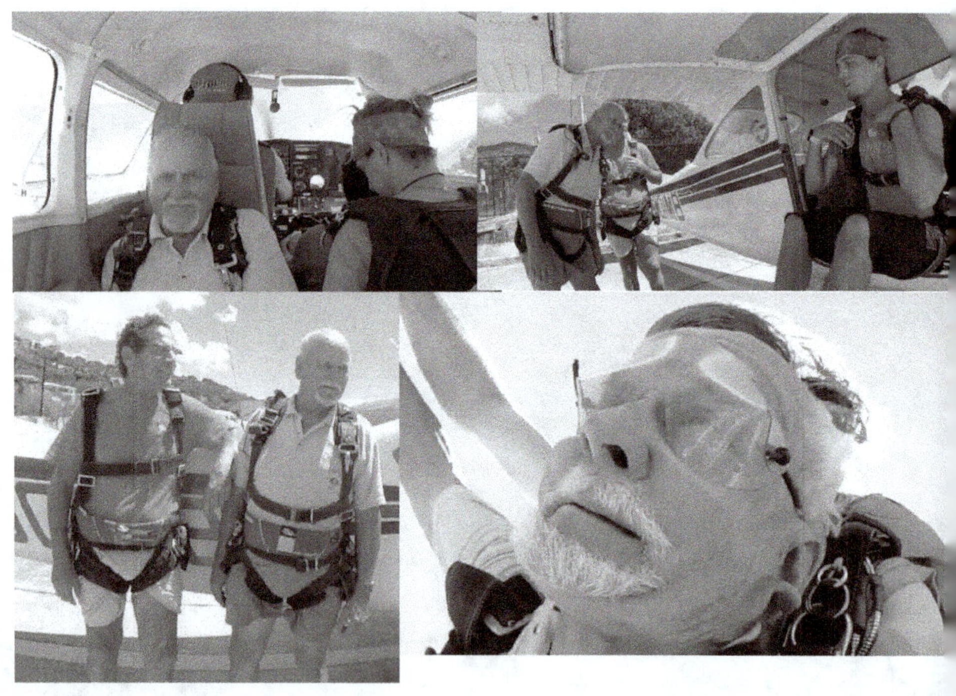

My father Captain Nels George Hagenson.
The main pilot of the DC-8 the entire time during the hijacking.

My hero.

Email all inquiries to thedoomsdayflight@gmail.com